an imprint of Penguin Random House LLC

375 Hudson Street

New York, New York 10014

First published in the UK by Ebury Press, 2017 as MODERN BAKER

Most Avery books are available at special quantity discounts for bulk purchase for sales promotions, premiums, fund-raising, and educational needs. Special books or book excerpts also can be created to fit specific needs. For details, write to SpecialMarkets@penguinrandomhouse.com.

ISBN 9780525533764

Printed in China.

10 9 8 7 6 5 4 3 2 1

Book design by Sandra Zellmer

The recipes contained in this book are to be followed exactly as written. The publisher is not responsible for your specific health or allergy needs that may require medical supervision. The publisher is not responsible for any adverse reactions to the recipes contained in this book.

super **loaves** & simple **treats**

Modern Baking for Healthier Living

MELISSA SHARP
WITH LINDSAY STARK

PAM KRAUSS BOOKS | AVERY
NEW YORK

009 INTRODUCTION

Melissa's Story 10

The Team 12

Healthy Eating 14

Healthy Baking 18

Sugar 21

Flour 22

027 BREADS

119 CAKES

229 COOKIES, BARS & BITES

Glossary 274

Index 277

Suppliers & Stockists 284

About Us 285

Thank You 288

modernbaker

INTRODUCTION

If you've become used to thinking cakes are bad, bread dangerous, and baking best kept as an indulgence, this book will be full of good news. It will transform your ideas and show you a revolutionary way to bake that is absolutely delicious and also good for you.

Modern Baker is a thriving bakery and café in Oxford, UK, where we make the healthiest breads and cakes it is humanly possible to produce that still taste delicious. All of our different breads are made with natural sourdough starters—our own wild yeast cultures made only from flour and water—teeming with beneficial lactobacilli bacteria. So our breads are made with just stone-ground flour, water, and fresh air and then long-fermented for 48 hours. Many of our cakes, cookies, and bars use these sourdough starters, too. Research shows that sourdough is great because it addresses the vitally important issue of helping to improve our gut health. It also naturally reduces Glycemic Index (GI) and gluten levels if using a natural sourdough culture and if it's long-fermented.

More people are realizing the importance of a healthy digestive system for our well-being. When the ingredients are combined to make sourdough they explode into the millions of fermenting microbes that our digestive tract is crying out for, vital elements of which survive through baking. This opens the door to a wealth of benefits that can transform our health.

Sourdough bread can be an everyday, health-giving delight, but who doesn't also love the occasional sweet treat? The way we make them at Modern Baker ensures that there is no reason not to enjoy these too. We only use unrefined ingredients to sweeten our treats, such as coconut sugar, dates, maple syrup, raw honey, and lucuma. Although evidence shows these are all better for you than the white sugar generally used in baking, they are nonetheless sugars and should still be regarded as treats. Coupled with stone-ground whole grains and as many nuts, seeds, fruits, and other nutritious ingredients as we can fit, baking has never been so good for you. Every ingredient earns its place according to our three core principles: good provenance, nutritional benefit, and great taste. Nothing is included just for the sake of it.

We believe passionately that it's possible to make wonderfully delicious cakes, cookies, and bars that also make a positive contribution to a healthy diet. What's more, the recipes are simple to make. There are no complicated directions here; you can rustle up a batch of something delicious in less than an hour. Finally, we can all have our cake and eat it, too!

All of our recipes are vegetarian and clearly marked with symbols to indicate which are gluten-free (GF), dairy-free (DF), or suitable for vegan (V+) diets.

This book is a labor of love, packed with fabulous recipes that are positively, proactively good for you—and, most importantly, simple to make and excellent to eat. The Danish concept of "hygge" holds that the value to the soul of making simple pleasures special is central to our well-being, so any food that ignores the pleasure principle is missing the point. Sometimes a slice of cake or a hot chocolate can be just the thing. It's no accident that the store embraces a fresh Nordic esthetic: hygge operates at its heart.

Before you get started on putting into practice the art, science, and miracle of natural fermentation in your own kitchen, find out how Melissa started on her transformative journey to becoming a Modern Baker.

MELISSA'S STORY

In January 2010, aged 36, I found a lump in my right breast. The consultant told me it was benign, but gave me the option to have it removed. My instinct told me I should, and that small procedure was the beginning of an incredible journey that changed my life. My lump turned out to be home to an aggressive, cancer. The full house of chemo- and radiotherapy was prescribed.

My new boyfriend, Leo, had been through his own bout of trauma and illness and had already adopted alternative, healthy ways of living. He immediately bought an organic cabbage, blitzed it, and encouraged me to drink it. Not long after, we were discussing the detoxing merits of coffee enemas, a topic I had never imagined ever discussing with anyone, let alone a partner! Very quickly I found myself talking to a number of alternative practitioners. Their advice was clear: supplementing my chemo with an array of natural supplements, organic green juices, and probiotics, cutting out dairy, and eating only grass-fed meat were all likely going to improve my body's ability to cope with the massive dose of toxins it was about to be hit with. I moved in with Leo.

Chemo was vile. It went on and on. But when a nurse asked how bad my mouth ulcers were I could say I had none, because I was drinking aloe vera four times a day, and she'd say, "Oh yes, I've heard of that before." At the end of my treatment I still had my hair, and when I explained it was because I hadn't washed it for nine weeks, some would take a step back, forgetting that shampoo is only one hundred years old. On the chemo ward the snack cart was always laden with sodas, candies, and cookies. I was just learning about the connections between sugar and cancer, and was shocked to see these things here of all places.

Finally my treatment ended. My nutritionist was clear that my postchemo routine, and my diet for the rest of my life, was even more important than during treatment. So, dutifully and gratefully, I kept my diet green, clean, and in control. I decided to immerse myself in it—and Leo came too.

Meanwhile, I had given up my stressful job as Operations Director in a management consultancy and halved my salary to work for a local, online organic supplements business. I packed boxes, did their social media, and started to increase my knowledge of nutrition. I discovered that not all sugars are equal and, shock-horror, nor are calories. Most scary of all, especially to someone who had spent much of her life fighting an eating disorder, I learned that some fats are positively good for you. This was just the start.

I began to apply my nutritional knowledge to my cooking at home, and a switch flicked on. I started writing online recipes for my job; they became really popular. What's more, I was eating like a horse but my weight remained stable.

I signed up for courses on nutrition and baking, and kept cooking for friends. When our local organic farm asked me to host a pop-up in their café for a weekend, I suddenly found myself faced with preparing a nutritious menu for one hundred and fifty people. I was petrified, but somehow I got through it—and found that I'd brought in over $2,500. That felt good. But so did the fact that my zucchini, corn, and chile fritters were gone in a flash. My quinoa patties had caused a stir, and several people had asked for seconds especially my zucchini chocolate cake served with homemade cashew nut cream.

It was at the farm café that I first appreciated how simple baking can be. Their bakery was the size of a backyard shed, with just three domestic ovens, one counter, and a dozen tubs of flours and seeds. The fact that it was always immaculate appealed to the dutiful side of me. The bread was the best I had ever eaten—and the sourdoughs were my favorite. It's amazing to think that back then I had no idea about the simple worlds natural fermentation that give sourdough its unique power.

I became determined to make this my business. As many people with my history do, I jumped in at the deep end, spending the next three years visiting organic bakeries, avant-garde delis, and restaurants everywhere—Scandinavia, Paris, New York, London—all in the interest of research. Our vacations became missions, and were all the more pleasurable for it.

We finally alighted on the concept of a café-bakery. I needed a professional baker to join me, and having scoured the country I found the wonderful Lindsay Stark, a graduate of the School of Artisan Food in Nottingham.

We decided to go as hard-core as anyone in the UK: long-fermented sourdough breads only (no added, commercial yeast), made with organic preindustrial, stone-ground grains of wheat, rye, and many others. Everything overrefined would be forbidden: our cakes, cookies, and pastries would be made only with unrefined sugars. Our proposition of healthy baking was born.

Since Modern Baker first exploded onto an appreciative community in Oxford, England, with our healthy baking concept, the UK government has awarded us a substantial two-year research and development funding grant to help bring our vision to the public. This sees us working with universities, food industry scientists, farmers, and millers to achieve the healthiest possible results. At the heart of it is a Model Gut System, which is a piece of equipment that mimics the human digestive system and allows us to test for all sorts of nutritional and health benefits. We have also invested in a new state-of-the-art bakery to put our sourdough baked goods into wider production to sell through other stores and online.

We love what we do. We're passionate about spreading the word that delicious, healthy bread and treats can nourish the soul as well as the body.

THE TEAM

Our team is growing all the time, becoming ever more international, but we started with a core of four.

I first advertised for a baker to fit into my concept of "healthy." When I met Lindsay, I was completely humbled to find someone who not only shared my concept but took it so much further. From her academic training at the UK's most prestigious Nottingham School of Artisan Food, she brought a knowledge of the miraculous properties of bacteria, yeast, and fungi that turned a handful of flour, salt, and water into a delicious, nutrition-packed loaf.

Another fortuitous find was Charlotte, who began making the coffee, but was soon writing our boards and revealing her talents as an art-school trained illustrator. We asked her to design an "urban forest" around the Modern Baker's storefront to represent the metaphor of healthy food at the center of a natural life, and her interpretation fast became a key part of our brand. Since then Charlotte's career has really taken off, recognized by a number of awards, with Modern Baker providing the ideal "starter culture."

Completing the team was Leo. Once a success in advertising, then with a portfolio of business interests and now pretty much exclusively dedicated to the growth of Modern Baker, his energy and vision is a critical driving force behind the scenes.

With healthy eating being such a vibrant sector, we're now inundated with resumés, often from thousands of miles away, and our rapidly expanding team is packed with passionate experts from all over the world (and a fair few devotees from the Oxford area). Each has had a part to play in bringing this book to life.

HEALTHY EATING

Should we count calories, are fats in or out, are supplements to be avoided, should we be eating more raw food? Well, yes and no—to all of these. Only a few decades ago, it wasn't this tricky. Shopping and eating was a simpler business. Our choices were more limited, and we knew instinctively what was good for us. We ate a greater variety of foods, and most of them were unprocessed and unrefined.

Now we are overwhelmed with both choice and advice. The relative merits of individual foods are revised constantly, alongside the even more complex science of how they react together. For example, adding butter to bread greatly lowers its Glycemic Index (GI) value, as the butter slows the body's insulin response. Then there's the matter of bioavailability. This has to do with how well our body is able to exploit the theoretical benefits of a particular substance.

OUR PHILOSOPHY

We have two simple views on how to deal with all this. First, the key thing we focus on isn't calories, or fats, or even sugars: it's GUT HEALTH. And second, we're all about the quality and provenance of our ingredients. Everything we use is as whole and unprocessed as it can be, with as little added as humanly possible. As the saying goes, stick to foods that your great-grandmother would have recognized and you won't go far wrong.

WHAT IS A HEALTHY GUT?

A healthy large intestine contains trillions of microbes that make up your gut flora, also known as your microbiome. This weighs up to an astonishing 4½ pounds. Like a garden, your microbiome needs to be tended. Processed, nutritionally poor foods offer no fuel for it; they effectively bypass it. The good kinds of microbes flourish when we eat a varied diet of the right kinds of foods, specifically those that contain prebiotics and probiotics. Prebiotics provide the fiber that nourishes the flora that are already there. Good examples include endive, artichokes, leeks, bananas, apples, and whole grains. Probiotics provide more live bacteria. Sourdough, sauerkraut, and yogurt are all natural probiotics.

WHY DOES A HEALTHY GUT MATTER?

A healthy gut is key to our overall health, both mental and physical. The gut is home to our enteric nervous system, sometimes referred to as the "second brain." Scientists now think that some 95 percent of our serotonin—a neurotransmitter essential to mood stability—is made in our digestive tract. Research shows that our digestive tract health plays a crucial role in controlling stress, anxiety, and even depression.

Our physical health is profoundly affected by our gut flora, too. About 80 percent of our immune system is our gut microbes, so to be healthy and fight off diseases our gut flora needs to be in championship shape. It processes the good nutrients in our food so they can be absorbed in the intestines and enter the blood. It also neutralizes harmful substances.

Our ancestors ate on average one hundred and fifty different ingredients each week; all whole foods, naturally rich in prebiotics and occasionally probiotics. Many people now eat fewer than twenty, mostly refined, which are often packed with chemicals and unrecognizable biologically from the foods we were eating just decades ago. It's hardly surprising that human health in the West is deteriorating.

WHAT CAN WE DO?

The good news is that it's not hard to change, and healthy baking can help. We should feel encouraged that our body is brilliantly made and resilient, and start to think about what we can do to change. When we know better, we do better. Every meal is another chance to nourish our body with good food. People are waking up to this; it's working; they tell others. It catches on. That's happening all around us.

There are four simple steps we can all take to greatly improve our diet, none of which are remotely controversial: reduce the amount of sugar we eat; increase the amount of fiber and whole foods; switch to foods with good provenance; and eat fermented foods. This books helps you achieve all four—with a generous helping of more-ishness.

HEALTHY BAKING

In the middle of the 20th century, refined white industrial flour began to dominate the baking scene. It slowly pushed out the sourdoughs made with stone-ground flours that had been our daily bread for millennia. Along with this came processes designed to speed up production built around industrial yeasts. The dough for factory-produced bread is proofed for less than an hour and laced with processing aids. Adding extra gluten is another shortcut, and one that is thought to have contributed to the widespread rise in gluten sensitivity. The result is a loaf low in nutritional value and, of course, taste. A million miles away from where it all started.

WHAT ABOUT SOURDOUGH?

A proper sourdough loaf is as good as it's always been. Long fermentation breaks down the carbohydrates and gluten in the grains, so many find the finished loaf is much easier to digest and the nutrients more easily absorbed. The result is healthy bread, packed with nutrients and bacteria created by the fermentation. One of nature's better miracles.

Another benefit of sourdough bread is that it has a lower glycemic index (GI), which means it doesn't cause the spike in our blood sugars that processed bread does. Then come the benefits for our gut health, partly from the fibrous stone-ground whole grains used to make the flour, and partly from the bacteria that results from fermentation, as some of the good bacteria remains after baking.

The only ingredients in a basic sourdough loaf are flour, water, and salt—and, crucially, time, to produce the carbon dioxide that makes the bread rise naturally (no artificial yeast is added). The lactic acid this produces is full of lactobacillus bacteria that create the familiar tangy, slightly sour flavor. They also make the vitamins and minerals in the flour easier for the body to absorb.

The best way of knowing your sourdough is healthy is to buy it from an authentic artisanal bakery or, even better, make it yourself. Some bread labeled as sourdough is really "sour-faux," made with an accelerated process that results in none of the healthy benefits. Like everything else in this book, ours is real—and transformative.

DELICIOUS AND NUTRITIOUS

Making bread and cakes the way we describe in this book gives them so much more flavor. With bread, the lactobacillus give that tangy flavor, but the true nature of the grain also comes through, whether it's wheat, rye, spelt, or kamut. It also gives it more body, so you need to eat less. One or two slices of the majority of breads in this book will leave most people feeling full. You can eat this delicious fermented food and feel full and well, without guilt.

In contrast to factory-produced, commercial breads, an authentic sourdough contains a whole host of nutrients. Vitamins B1-B6, B12, folate, thiamine, niacin, riboflavin, vitamin E, selenium, iron, manganese, calcium, magnesium, phosphorus, zinc, potassium, balanced proteins, and fatty acids are all examples of what many good sourdough breads can contain.

LESS WASTE

We've all fallen into the habit of buying more than we can use. Happily with our foods this tends not to be a problem. The long fermentation of sourdough slows the processes that make bread go stale. As a result, your delicious, healthy loaf retains much of its moisture and lasts longer. A week-old loaf (yes, they can last that long) is in fact better for toast, for example, while the flavor of a carrot cake develops in intensity over time. Once you start on this journey of healthy baking, your garbage cans will be much lighter for it.

Incidentally, our bread freezes brilliantly, too. Many of our customers slice and freeze a range of breads, so they're readily available for different occasions.

SO DOES IT COST MORE?

With bread, not really. All the basic loaves in this book will cost less in ingredients than a cheap loaf in a grocery store, last twice as long, and contain a compelling list of health benefits—and taste much, much better.

When it comes to healthy cakes and cookies, yes. Coconut oil costs more than butter, maple syrup and honey costs more than white sugar, and raw cacao is more expensive than prepared cocoa powder. What price do you put on health? And by the time you add up the other less obvious benefits of staying fuller longer, less waste, and much tastier baking, in our humble view, the extra cost isn't what it seems.

SUGAR

Our customers love the purity of our bread, but what generates more discussion and excitement, and more buzz on social media, is the fact that we don't use any refined sugars in our cakes and other sweet treats.

Our philosophy on sugar is really very simple. We only use unrefined sugars. We're quite fussy about which ones we use and we use them as sparingly as we can get away with, using fruit wherever possible. There are three reasons why we are firmly against using refined sugars and artificial sweeteners. First, research shows that they play havoc with gut bacteria. Second, they cause blood sugar and insulin levels to soar. And third, they contain no nutrients or fiber; they are empty calories.

NATURAL SUGARS

Natural sugars contain more nutrients than refined versions, and fruits add fiber. They also bring some wonderfully rich flavors to your baking.

Healthy baking also means significantly less sweetness overall, and this is a plus because it allows other flavors to emerge. This makes the use of other carefully selected ingredients even more worthwhile and opens up whole new dimensions for baking.

The natural sugars we use are still sugars, however, and they should still be regarded as a treat. Your taste buds will quickly become attuned to how sweet many supposedly "unsweet" foods are, and appreciate all the other wonderful flavors available.

Time to start experimenting!

FLOUR

We use stone-ground flour. This means that the grain is ground between two stones. It creates flour with much more flavor and better nutrition, because it retains some of the bran and the germ of the grain. Commercially made bread mostly uses flour that has lost its bran and germ during the milling process.

WHEAT

Wheat is the most commonly used grain in bread baking. A wheat grain is made up of three separate parts: the outside that includes the bran, the germ at the heart of the grain, and the endosperm, which is the storehouse containing the starch and the proteins that make gluten. The gluten gives the lightness of structure to wheat bread.

In many of our breads we use a strong wheat flour, but softer wheats are better for cakes and cookies.

RYE

Rye was once a widely grown grain in the UK, but less so now. It still thrives in the colder climates of northeastern Europe, so these areas have become known for their dark, dense rye breads. Rye flour is available as light, medium, or dark according to the amount of bran in it; we prefer to use the light flour.

Rye does contain gluten, so isn't suitable for celiacs, but it contains less gluten than wheat so it makes a more dense loaf.

KAMUT

Kamut is an ancient form of wheat from Egypt. It was pushed out of cultivation for a long time, but is now seeing a resurgence in popularity. It was originally called khorasan but the name was changed to kamut (an ancient Egyptian word for "wheat"). It has a rich, buttery taste and a slightly grainy texture. It is appearing increasingly in products such as pasta, couscous, and granola. It is slightly higher in protein, potassium, and magnesium than traditional wheat, and can be better for those who are gluten intolerant.

SPELT

Spelt is an ancient grain, high in fiber, and a source of protein. It is easier to digest than wheat flour because its gluten is more water soluble. Spelt bread is more dense than wheat bread but less dense than rye. Its mellow flavor is great for people new to sourdough bread. We use a rye starter in our spelt sourdough, so it is free from standard wheat.

Spelt also works really well in place of soft flours in cake baking, and is what we use in our nongluten-free cakes.

SPROUTED WHOLE WHEAT

In sprouted whole wheat flour the whole grain is soaked in a small amount of water, which makes it start to grow. It releases enzymes that make the nutrients in it more easily absorbed by the body.

Organic
Stoneground
Gluten Free
1kg
BuyWholeFoodsOnline.co.uk
0800 0431 455
Suma
Quality
PSYLLIUM
Suma
Quality
TAPIOCA
FLOUR
500g
The Finest in Natural Foods

GLUTEN-FREE FLOURS

BUCKWHEAT

Buckwheat isn't actually a form of wheat at all; it's related to the rhubarb family. It's a minor crop in the USA, but it has been used for centuries in Russia to make kasha, in Brittany to make pancakes, and Japan for soba noodles. It has a nutty, slightly bitter flavor and is packed with the antioxidant rutin.

TEFF

Teff grains are absolutely tiny, so no matter what teff flour you get (brown, white, or red) it will be whole grain, as it is too small to mill. Teff has a slightly molasses-like flavor and is much richer in calcium than most other grains. It's the main source of nutrition in Ethiopia.

TAPIOCA AND POTATO

These two flours play more or less the same role in gluten-free baking. They have little in the way of flavor or nutritional value, but they're important for producing a binding, cohesive effect in our gluten-free sourdough breads, making them lighter.

QUINOA

Quinoa has increased in popularity exponentially in recent years. It is a seed that is famed for being a complete protein that can be used as a replacement for grains like rice. We also like to use quinoa flour and flakes in our bread. It has a slightly nutty and bitter flavor.

BROWN RICE

Our gluten-free starter is made of rice flour and water. We use a brown rice flour because it produces a really lively starter. It has quite a bitter taste and a grainy texture, so it works best mixed with other flours.

CHICKPEA

Also known as gram flour, chickpea flour is a source of protein, magnesium, iron, folate, and copper. It has a binding effect and a strong, savory flavor, which is why we combine it with other, milder flours such as buckwheat, potato, and tapioca in our chickpea sourdough.

Breads

Lindsay is our head baker, a key member of our team who brings endless expertise and creativity to our work.

She was introduced to baking at a young age, like so many people, at home in the kitchen with her mom, but never thought it would become her career. After a degree in linguistics she worked in academic publishing, but she didn't find it very fulfilling.

Lindsay had read somewhere that the thing you do while you procrastinate is what you should be doing as your job. She realized she spent most of her free time deciding what she was going to bake—she even had a complicated color-coded spreadsheet of her plans! And so she enrolled at the School of Artisan Food on the Welbeck Estate in Nottingham, UK, on a comprehensive course in professional baking. This is where she fell in love with the simplicity of sourdough: just three ingredients combined to create something that far surpasses its humble origins. That fascination has never left her.

Lindsay also began to realize how much poor-quality bread and lazy baking there is out there, and how bad for you factory-produced bread can be. She was shocked by the amount of sugar there is in the patisserie treats we all enjoy. After her course, and a stint at a bakery in Bristol, she found her way to Modern Baker. The fit was perfect, it felt like the job had been created just for her. It's important to Lindsay that we make food that everyone can enjoy—foodies who love great bread, people with dietary needs, cake lovers, and healthy eating buffs. Food is as much about the comfort and pleasure it gives us as it is about nourishing our bodies. If it feels like a chore to eat, then how much good can it really be doing you?

BASIC TECHNIQUES

All the recipes yield a single loaf. To make two or more loaves, multiply the ingredients accordingly, including the starter, and divide the dough before shaping it.

MEASURING INGREDIENTS

It is important in baking to measure ingredients carefully and a digital scale is ideal for this. In the bakery we even weigh our water because it's far more accurate than using measuring cups, so all the measures in this Bread section are also in grams.

KEEPING ONE HAND CLEAN

A good baker always keeps one hand clean, in case you need to grab something as you're working. You can also use the clean hand to get bits off the other one.

FOLDING AND RISING

You want to develop a light touch when handling your bread dough. It's your friend, after all; there's no need to grapple with it. Rough handling will make it more sticky, and more likely to tear. You want to achieve a smooth texture that is reasonably firm. It won't take you long to get the hang of it; it's all about practice and a bit of confidence.

When most people think of making bread they think of kneading dough. The purpose of kneading is to develop the gluten in the dough, but there's another way and it's the one we use in the bakery. It's a technique of folding and leaving the dough to rise slowly. The gluten is activated when water is added to the flour.

Having made the dough and left it to rest for 5- to 10-minutes on a lightly floured counter, transfer to a bowl, and fold it in gently from the outside to the middle all the way around, so four or five folds. We do this four times, with 5 to 10 minute rests between each set of folds. After this the dough is an even, squarish shape. Leave it, covered with a damp dish towel, for an hour to stop it drying out.

Now the active agents in the dough—the yeast and the bacteria—start to go to work, eating the sugars in the flour. Yeast and bacteria are a lot like humans—they like to be warm, and they like to be fed. The flour provides the food, and room temperature the warmth, which keeps them on an even keel, respiring and consuming the sugars. As they eat they produce gas, which makes an open texture in the bread, and acid, which gives the bread its sour taste. The acid also breaks down the gluten. This is why bread made from sourdough that has had a long proofing time is easier to digest than bread that is made quickly—and crucially it also has a deeper, richer flavor.

After an hour, it's time to fold the dough again; this is also sometimes known as knocking back. The reason we do this is to align the gluten strands so that then it will trap the air bubbles better. This gives a more even result. We've all cut into a loaf to find an enormous gaping hole in the middle of our slice, which is not what you want. The second, important reason for folding the dough is to redistribute the heat evenly. As the yeast and bacteria feed they generate heat. The center of the dough will be hotter than the outside. Let it rest for another hour.

SHAPING

After an hour, preshape the dough. This is vital if you are making a batch of loaves as it creates a good starting shape to begin the final shape from, giving you a more consistent loaf overall. If you are baking a single loaf, as we do in the recipes, then you might choose to leave this step out as your dough will already be in a round shape from the resting bowl.

Preshaping is done with both hands. The left hand doesn't move; it's like the Sun to your right hand's Earth. It cups the dough as you turn it with the other hand. Your right hand moves swiftly and evenly around the ball of dough, curling it under and pressing down as it goes around. This tightens the surface of the dough, too. The trick is to do it quickly, or your hands will stick. Then we let it rest again for 5 to 10 minutes, seam side up.

The final shaping depends on whether you're going for a "rustic" loaf shape or baking it in a pan. See the recipes for which method to use.

If you are shaping a long rustic loaf, turn the dough out onto a lightly floured counter and stretch it out into a long, flattened oval shape, using both hands. Take one end of the dough and fold it into the middle. Repeat with the other end, so it now resembles a rectangle. The two ends should overlap a little in the middle.

Pull and fold the top of the rectangle in toward you so that it covers a third of the way down. Tuck the dough in with your thumbs.

Repeat until you have a sausage shape. Roll it to tighten it slightly and make it as even as possible.

OVERNIGHT PROOFING

The shaped dough is then left to proof overnight. In the bakery we use a cool retarder cabinet, but a refrigerator does just the same job. What you're after is a slow rise. This allows the dough to develop flavor and pre-digest more of the gluten in its fermentation. If you want to speed things up, you can leave the dough in a warm place for 2 to 4 hours instead, until it has more or less doubled in size, then bake straightaway.

SCORING

This is the last thing to do before putting your precious loaf in the oven. And it must be just before it goes in—don't do it then take a phone call for 10 minutes, or the dough will lose too much gas. We like to use a small sharp knife with a slightly serrated blade. Be definite about it and score the dough in one continuous sweep, don't saw at it. We make a single diagonal slash down the loaf, about ½ inch deep and at an angle, but there are endless variations you can use—be creative, define your own distinctive pattern.

TEMPERATURE

You will find as you do more baking that the weather, and the temperature in your kitchen, will affect your dough. This isn't really surprising. When it's very warm, the yeast and bacteria in the dough become more active, so they eat more of the sugars in the flour and produce more gas and acid. These break down the gluten, so if the process goes too far there won't be enough gluten to give the bread structure and it will turn out flat. On a very cold day, on the other hand, the yeast and bacteria may not get warm enough to get to work on the flour sugars.

There is an ideal, called basic temperature, for this process: the sum of the temperature of the flour, of the air in the room, and of the water you add should be 140°F. The easiest of these three elements to change, to achieve the ideal temperature, is the water. If you want to be really precise about it you could use a probe thermometer to measure the temperature of the flour, and an ordinary one for the air, and so work out the best temperature for the water. In practice you'll find this is only really helpful in extremes of hot or cold. On a very hot day, use cold water and vice versa. It's also worth covering the dough with a damp dish towel to stop it drying out, or spraying it with a fine mist.

After you've been baking for a while, you'll get a feel for the water temperature you need. In normal conditions we use warm water, which we like to think of as "warm enough to swim in but not to have a bath in."

All this may seem a bit technical, but it soon becomes instinctive. Understanding a bit about the chemistry going on in the dough will give you the confidence to play around and experiment.

GLUTEN-FREE AND RYE BREADS

For gluten-free flours, of course, there is no need for all this folding, as there is no gluten being broken down. We simply mix the dough and leave it before putting it in a pan and smoothing over the surface. It's more like making a cake.

Although rye flour does contain gluten, it develops differently, so it requires the same treatment at this stage as a gluten-free flour.

BAKING

To tell if a loaf is baked, tap the bottom. If you're baking a loaf in a pan, you will obviously have to take it out of the pan for this. The bottom should sound hollow. If it doesn't, put it back in the oven for another 5 minutes. All ovens are different, but you will soon get to know how yours behaves. Let the bread cool out of the pan otherwise the bread will sweat and become soggy.

EQUIPMENT

SCRAPERS

The single most useful tool for the home baker is the plastic dough scraper. These come in different shapes and sizes, to suit the amount of dough you are handling. You can also buy a metal one with squared edges and a handle—this is called a bench scraper. The straight edge is useful for dividing up large quantities of dough into even-size pieces for making multiple loaves or rolls.

BOWLS

A good set of bowls is a must. These can be plastic, ceramic, or stainless steel. It's helpful if the bowls have lids, but you can also use a shower cap or dish towel to cover the bowl.

SPOONS

Wooden spoons are best for beating, metal spoons are best for folding. You will also need a spatula for scraping mixtures out of bowls.

PROOFING BASKETS

There are wicker or bamboo baskets available that give an attractive pattern to the loaf, and some of these are lined with cloth. A 2¼-pound proofing basket is the right size for these recipes. A plastic bowl or rectangular container lined with a dish towel would do just as well.

DISH TOWELS

A good supply of clean dish towels are needed to cover the dough while it is resting.

SCALE

A digital scale is essential, as accuracy is very important in baking. It's better to weigh liquids as well as solid ingredients, as it's more precise.

BAKING PANS

Choose good sturdy ones, especially for bread, where the baking temperature is very high. Loaf pans come in 1-pound and 2-pound capacities. For cakes we mostly use 9-inch round, 4-inch deep cake pans. For raw cakes, springform pans make it easier to remove the cake.

KNIFE

For scoring loaves before they go in the oven, a small, sharp knife with a slightly serrated blade is best.

THERMOMETER

You can use a digital thermometer to check the temperature of your ingredients.

FOOD PROCESSOR

This can be useful for making some cakes, especially a carrot cake, though often it's just as easy to mix it by hand. You won't need more than the standard blade and grater disk.

ELECTRIC BEATERS OR WHISK

Useful for quick whipping and beating egg whites.

HIGH-SPEED BLENDER

Machines with powerful engines, such as the Nutribullet or Vitamix, are useful for chopping ingredients such as nuts very finely and blending toppings and fillings. You can use a standard blender, but the result will be less smooth.

OTHER KITCHEN STAPLES

Wire racks, wax paper, and parchment paper, cutting boards, measuring cups, scissors, rolling pin, and a roasting pan.

MAKING YOUR SOURDOUGH STARTER

A sourdough starter is a method for cultivating wild yeast in a form that can be used for baking that has been used for thousands of years. A sourdough starter is also known as a levain, and sometimes a mother (because it keeps producing babies).

The starter is the magic, the genius, at the heart of everything we do and everything in this book. It's an ancient technology, discovered by accident and passed from generation to generation. It forms the basis of transformational foods with unbelievable powers of preservation and flavor.

A lot of people are intimidated by the idea of making and keeping a starter, but it really doesn't need to be daunting and is in fact something a child could do. Getting a starter going takes 2 minutes a day, over 5 days. It's really not that much effort at all. The easiest way to make one is simply to combine flour and warm water and let the mixture sit for several days. In theory, you will only need to do this once, and your starter will be unique to you. If you use it on a regular basis, maintaining it just becomes part of your bread and baking routine, and if you do not use it as regularly, or you're going on vacation and are worried about leaving it for a while, don't be. It can cope!

Keep your starter in the refrigerator unless you are using it every day. Bring it out to top it off, then return it when you have finished using it in your recipes. It will be fine there even for a few months without being used. It may separate, but don't panic, just mix it back together. To get it going again you want to really overwhelm it with food. So throw half of it away and add ¾ cup (100 g) flour and 7 tablespoons (100 g) warm water.

Leave it out at room temperature overnight, and the next day it should be active again, i.e., bubbling away. It really is that straightforward. At this stage you could use it, but we would recommend throwing half of it away again and topping it off with however much you need for your recipe. By throwing half of the starter away you also throw away half of the microorganisms so they each get more food. This will make the starter more active more quickly. We find that by taking that one extra day with a rejuvenated starter you get a much more active starter, resulting in a better flavor and rise in your bread.

In the bakery we have three bread starters: wheat, rye, and brown rice for gluten-free baking. For our basic sourdough we use the wheat starter. This has an almost cheesy smell to it and a slightly more mellow flavor than the rye starter.

WHEAT STARTER

EQUIPMENT
A container with a lid or a clean jar.

DAY 1

- 1 teaspoon (5 g) white bread flour
- 1 teaspoon (5 g) warm water, (90 to 99°F)

Mix together the flour and the water in a container with a lid. We recommend mixing with your hands rather than a spoon. We all have naturally occurring yeasts on our hands, so this can give your starter a real boost.

Leave the mixture overnight at room temperature. Cover it with the lid but do not make it airtight. A screw-top jar with the lid partly done up is perfect. You want the yeasts in the air to get in, but you also want to prevent the mixture from drying out.

DAY 2

- Wheat starter made on Day 1
- 1 teaspoon (5 g) white bread flour
- 1 teaspoon (5 g) warm water, (90 to 99°F)

Throw away half of the mixture from Day 1. This is because you want to almost overwhelm the bacteria/yeast in the starter with food, by adding more flour than the weight of the original mixture. You could do this by adding more flour and warm water and not throwing any away, but you would very quickly end up with an excessively large amount of starter.

Stir the flour and water into the remaining mix and leave again at room temperature overnight.

DAYS 3 AND 4
Repeat Day 2.

DAY 5
By now you should notice your starter has bubbles in it. This means it is ready! Don't worry if it smells acidic or cheesy, this is completely normal and each starter will create its own unique fragrance. Now you have your own living, bubbling jar of healthy microbes that you'll be using for years to come.

HOW TO USE YOUR STARTER IN BAKING
With your active starter, you're ready to start sourdough baking. The first thing to remember is that to make a sourdough recipe you will need to build up your active starter (using all of it) the day before you bake. This is detailed in each recipe under the heading of Day 1.

Having built your starter up, you will need to use most of it for the recipe (in the recipe we refer to it as the Recipe starter). What you don't use, you retain as your ongoing active starter for your next recipe—you don't want to have to start from scratch each time! This all sounds more confusing than it really is.

TROUBLESHOOTING
If the starter isn't obviously bubbling, keep repeating Day 2 until it does bubble. Quite a few factors can affect how long it takes a starter to activate, temperature being one of the main ones. If you begin your starter in cold conditions it may take longer to get going. Also, the general environment can have an impact. In the bakery, as we are making bread every day, there is so much yeast in the atmosphere that we find starters can take just a few days to get going, whereas if a kitchen is more sterile, it's likely to take much longer.

RYE STARTER

A rye starter has a unique flavor, completely different from the wheat starter. It's more acidic, or vinegary, than cheesy. The texture is also quite different because the rye absorbs more water, so it will be thicker.

Follow the Wheat starter steps for Day 1 to Day 5, using 1 teaspoon rye flour instead of white bread flour.

GLUTEN-FREE BROWN RICE STARTER

Making a gluten-free starter is exactly the same as making a standard one. The only ingredients are gluten-free flour and warm water. We use brown rice flour as it produces a really lively starter, but you can use almost any gluten-free flour. Teff, for example, gives a more acidic flavor.

The only gluten-free flours we don't recommend using for the starter are buckwheat, potato, and tapioca flour. The smell of a buckwheat starter is one that will haunt you, and not in the way that the smell of a freshly baked loaf can haunt you! It's quite likely to make you wish you didn't have a sense of smell! Potato and tapioca flour have a different problem. Because they are essentially a starch, they absorb a lot of water, so if you leave a flour-and-water mixture overnight it will form quite a solid block. This won't have enough fluidity to form the necessary bubbles and activity that are needed in a starter. You can get around this by using more water, but that can affect the final loaf.

Follow the Wheat starter steps for Day 1 to Day 5, using 1 teaspoon brown rice flour or another gluten-free flour instead of the white bread flour. However, on Day 1 use 2 teaspoons water, but from Day 2 to Day 5 revert back to 1 teaspoon water.

MODERN BAKER BASIC SOURDOUGH

MAKES 1 loaf **EQUIPMENT** 2-pound loaf pan **DF** **V+**

This is our basic bread recipe—Modern Baker long-fermented sourdough. It is a really simple loaf with just four ingredients—wheat flour, rye flour, water, and salt. We use a small amount of rye flour in the mix to give a subtle extra dimension to the flavor. It's crusty with an open crumb, and its color is quite dark and earthy, really not what you'd expect a white loaf to look like. Because it has no added yeast it's naturally dense, but this is how bread has been made since time immemorial. After eating a proper long-fermented sourdough bread, most people never look back.

I love this loaf; it's the closest I can get to memories of the natural food I enjoyed at my grandparents' house. And it goes with anything—it makes fabulous toast and it's great for tartines. What's more, it will keep for a week and can be frozen.

As well as being one of our most popular loaves in its own right, this is also the basis for many of our weekend specials as it's very easy to adapt. We have included some of our favorite varieties here, but why not experiment for yourself? Once you've mastered the routines of making this loaf, all other breadmaking will be straightforward and simple.

This recipe describes how to shape the bread as a long rustic-shaped loaf using a proofing basket, but it could just as easily be made in a pan (see Sprouted Whole Wheat Sourdough for doing this, page 66). Generally, rustic is a good shape for sharing at the table, whereas one in a pan has a thinner crust and tighter crumb, and is excellent for sandwiches and toast.

ADDITIONAL EQUIPMENT YOU WILL NEED FOR THIS AND MOST BREAD RECIPES

- Weighing scale (preferably digital)
- 2 large mixing bowls
- Plastic dough scraper
- Dish towel or shower cap
- Proofing basket
- 1 flat baking sheet and 1 rimmed baking sheet or roasting pan
- Small sharp knife

DAY 1

- 6 tablespoons (50 g) white bread flour
- 3½ tablespoons (50 g) warm water, (90 to 99°F)
- Active Wheat Starter (page 41)

Mix the flour and water with the whole quantity of the starter and leave loosely covered at room temperature overnight.

DAY 2

- 3½ ounces (100 g) recipe starter from Day 1
- 1½ cups (375 g) warm water (90 to 99°F)
- 3¼ cups (450 g) white bread flour
- ½ cup (50 g) light rye flour
- 1½ teaspoons (8 g) salt

NUTRITION NOTE

This is the loaf that our local university persuaded us to do a GI test on. The result was, as expected, a GI much lower than its nonsourdough counterpart.

1 On Day 2, in a large bowl combine the recipe starter with the warm water and mix gently. If it's colder the dough will take a long time to proof, and if it's too warm it is likely to over proof and lose its open structure. As a guide, it should feel warm enough to swim in, but too cold to have a bath in!

2 In another bowl, combine the two flours and the salt. Always mix the salt into the dry flour, as salt will kill the active agents, the bacteria and yeast, if you put it in later.

3 Add the flour mix to the first bowl and mix using one hand until a dough forms. This takes only a couple of minutes. It's a good idea to use only one hand, leaving the other one clean for using utensils, etc. Use a plastic dough scraper around the bowl to make sure all the flour is mixed in. Cover the bowl with a shower cap or damp dish towel and let it rest at room temperature.

4 After 5 to 10 minutes, give the dough a fold in the bowl. Use slightly wet hands to prevent the dough sticking to them. Pull a section of the dough out to the side and fold it into the middle of the ball. Repeat this going around the ball of dough until you get back to the beginning (four or five folds). Use the scraper to turn the dough upside down, cover the bowl, and leave for another 5 to 10 minutes. Repeat this three times.

After the final fold, cover the bowl again and let it rest for 1 hour at room temperature.

5 Turn the dough out of the bowl onto a lightly floured counter. Stretch out one side of the dough and fold it into the middle. Repeat this with each of the four "sides" of the dough. Put the dough back in the bowl upside down and let rest for another hour.

6 **Shaping a long rustic loaf:** Turn the dough out onto a lightly floured counter and stretch it out into a long, flattened oval shape, using both hands. Take one end of the dough and fold it into the middle. Repeat with the other end, so that the dough now resembles a rectangle. The two ends should overlap a little in the middle.

Pull and fold the top of the rectangle in toward you so that it covers a third of the way down. Tuck the dough in with your thumbs.

Repeat this until you have a sausage shape. Roll it to tighten it slightly and make the shape as even as possible.

7 Lightly flour an oval proofing basket and place the dough in it with the seam facing up and the smooth side on the bottom. We use unlined baskets as they give an attractive pattern on the final loaf.

8. In the bakery at this point we put the dough in our cool retarder cabinet for it to proof slowly overnight. This helps it to develop more flavor and become even healthier as it "predigests" more of the gluten and ferments even more probiotic qualities. Your version of our retarder is your refrigerator—and you can leave the proofing basket in it overnight, covered with the dish towel or shower cap. Take it out as you are heating the oven. It's fine for it to go in cold.

   However, if you would prefer to speed things up a little, at this stage you can simply leave the dough in a warm place (ideally 75°F) until it has more or less doubled in size. This should take 2 to 4 hours. To test when the dough has proofed enough, press your finger about ¾ to 1¼ inches into it, then remove. If the dough pushes back out slowly it is ready. If it springs back quickly it is underproofed; if it doesn't spring back at all, it is overproofed. There isn't much you can do about that. The bread will be edible, but more liable to collapse.

9. Preheat the oven to 480°F or the highest temperature on your oven. Place a roasting pan in the bottom of the oven to heat up. Fill a cup with water and place to one side ready to use. Also put a flat baking sheet in the oven to heat up.

10. When the oven is up to temperature, take the hot baking sheet out, lightly dust it with flour, and then turn the dough from the proofing basket out onto the sheet. Slash the dough with a sharp knife. Make sure that when you slash you use one quick, smooth action; do not saw at the dough. This will give you a much cleaner line. In the bakery we make a single diagonal slash down the loaf, but there are endless variations you could use—be creative, define your own distinctive pattern.

11. Place the baking sheet in the oven and pour the glass of water into the preheated roasting pan. The moisture from this makes the dough lighter, helps to set the crust, and gives it a lovely sheen.

12. Turn the temperature down to 465°F and bake for approximately 30 minutes. To check if the bread is baked through, tap the bottom—it should sound hollow.

13. Let the bread cool for at least an hour before eating. If you eat it when it's still hot, it will not have settled and so will be more difficult to digest.

MULTISEED SOURDOUGH

≡

This is the most popular loaf at the bakery. It has a devoted following among regular customers—one family buys ten at a time for their freezer!—and the most frequent first loaf for new customers. It's also popular with the restaurants we sell through. It is earthy and honest with primal qualities, no doubt the second leavened bread made by man.

Under any analysis, made with well-sourced ingredients this loaf is as healthy as it gets, with the seeds providing a protein hit as well as extra fiber and layers of extra flavors. Yet despite all this goodness and history, it's still an everyday loaf that every member of your family will enjoy.

We make this in both a pan and a round shape. These directions are for the round loaf, but you can use any of the alternative shaping directions from other recipes.

DAY 1

- 6 tablespoons (50 g) white bread flour
- 3½ tablespoons (50 g) warm water (90 to 99°F)
- Active Wheat Starter (see page 41)

Mix the flour and water with the whole quantity of the starter and leave loosely covered at room temperature overnight.

- ¼ cup (35 g) sunflower seeds
- ¼ cup (35 g) pumpkin seeds
- ¼ cup (35 g) golden flaxseeds
- 5 teaspoons (15 g) sesame seeds
- 1½ cups (335 g) warm water (90 to 99°F)

Soak the seeds in the water and leave at room temperature overnight.

DAY 2

- 3½ ounces (100 g) recipe starter from Day 1
- Water and seed mix from Day 1 (above)
- 2⅓ cups (335 g) white bread flour
- ⅓ cup (40 g) dark or light rye flour
- 1½ teaspoons (8 g) salt
- Extra seeds, for topping

NUTRITION NOTE

We soak the seeds for a couple of reasons. The first is to do with the bread-making process. If you don't soak the seeds they will absorb water from the dough, resulting in a drier dough and a heavier texture in the bread. So soaking the seeds guarantees a much more consistent loaf. The other benefit is that you activate them, which makes them release additional nutrients so that they are easier for your body to absorb.

MAKES 1 loaf **EQUIPMENT** round proofing basket **DF** **V+**

1 In a large bowl, combine the recipe starter with the water and seeds and mix gently.

2 In another bowl, combine the two flours and the salt.

3 Add the flour mix to the first bowl and mix using one hand until a dough forms. This takes only a couple of minutes. It's a good idea to use only one hand, leaving the other one clean for using utensils, etc. Use a plastic dough scraper around the bowl to make sure all the flour is mixed in. Cover the bowl with a shower cap or damp dish towel and let it rest at room temperature.

4 After 5 to 10 minutes, give the dough a fold in the bowl. Use slightly wet hands to prevent the dough sticking to them. Pull a section of the dough out to the side and fold it into the middle of the ball. Repeat this going around the ball of dough until you get back to the beginning (four or five folds). Use the scraper to turn the dough upside down, cover the bowl, and leave for another 5 to 10 minutes. Repeat this three times. After the final fold, cover the bowl again and let rest for 1 hour at room temperature.

5 Turn the dough out of the bowl onto a lightly floured counter. Stretch out one side of the dough and fold it into the middle. Repeat this with each of the four "sides" of the dough. Put the dough back in the bowl upside down and let rest for another hour at room temperature.

6 **Shaping a round loaf:** Once the dough has rested, turn it out onto a lightly floured counter. Stretch one side of the dough out and fold it into the middle. Repeat this all around the outside of the dough until you get back to your starting point. Flip it so the seam side is facing down. Use your left hand to hold the dough in place and use your right hand to rotate the dough, tucking it under and tightening it as you go around (if you are left-handed you might want to use your right hand to stabilize and your left hand to rotate). The idea here is to increase the strength of the dough without tearing it. The final surface of the dough should be taut to the touch.

7 Put the remaining seeds in a bowl. Brush the top of the dough with water and dunk it in the seeds so that they are evenly spread over the top. Place the dough so that the seam is facing up and the seeds face down in a round proofing basket. There is no need to flour the basket as the layer of seeds will prevent the dough from sticking.

8 Follow the rest of the Basic Sourdough recipe from Step 8 (page 44) to the end.

WALNUT SOURDOUGH

MAKES 1 loaf

EQUIPMENT oval proofing basket

DF V+

☰

Walnut sourdough is a perennially popular loaf that works with a whole range of dishes. Walnuts are often overlooked as a nut in favor of the more fashionable almonds, cashews, and macadamias, but they are incredibly nutritious. Whole wheat flour is a brown flour with an earthy flavor that pairs really well with the walnuts and gives this loaf its distinctive dark hue. We love this served very fresh with a big lump of cheddar and a few slices of apple.

DAY 1

- 6 tablespoons (50 g) white bread flour
- 3½ tablespoons (50 g) warm water (90 to 99°F)
- Active Wheat Starter (page 41)

Mix the flour and water with the whole quantity of the starter and leave loosely covered at room temperature overnight.

DAY 2

- 3½ ounces (100 g) recipe starter from Day 1
- 1¼ cups (325 g) warm water (90 to 99°F)
- 1¾ cups (250 g) white bread flour
- 1¾ cups (250 g) whole wheat flour
- 1½ teaspoons (8 g) salt
- ¾ cup (100 g) walnuts, coarsely chopped

1. In a large bowl, combine the recipe starter with the warm water and mix gently.
2. In another bowl, combine the two flours and the salt.
3. Add the flour mix to the first bowl and mix using one hand until a dough forms. This takes only a couple of minutes. It's a good idea to use only one hand, leaving the other one clean for using utensils, etc. Use a plastic dough scraper around the bowl to make sure all the flour is mixed in. Cover the bowl with a shower cap or damp dish towel and let it rest.
4. After 5 to 10 minutes, give the dough a fold in the bowl. Use slightly wet hands to prevent the dough sticking to them. Pull a section of the dough out to the side and fold it into the middle of the ball. Repeat this going around the ball of dough until you get back to the beginning (four or five folds). Use the scraper to turn the dough upside down, cover the bowl, and leave for another 5 to 10 minutes. Repeat this another two times. Add the walnuts and fold once more.
5. Turn the dough out of the bowl onto a lightly floured counter. Stretch out one side of the dough and fold it into the middle. Repeat this with each of the four "sides" of the dough. Put the dough back in the bowl upside down and let rest for another hour.
6. Follow the rest of the Basic Sourdough recipe from Step 6 (page 46) to the end.

OLIVE AND FETA SOURDOUGH

≡

This weekend treat is almost a meal in itself and a true "statement" loaf. The flavors conjure up the Mediterranean, and whereas lots of interesting ingredients change appearance during cooking, both the feta and the olives sit beautifully in this loaf, peeping through the crust.

DAY 1

- 1/4 cup (35 g) white bread flour
- 2 tablespoons (35 g) warm water (90 to 99°F)
- Active Wheat Starter (page 41)

Add the flour and water to the whole quantity of the starter and leave loosely covered overnight at room temperature.

DAY 2

- 2½ ounces (70 g) recipe starter from Day 1
- 1 cup (250 g) warm water (90 to 99°F)
- 2 cups (300 g) white bread flour
- 1/4 cup (35 g) light rye flour
- 1 teaspoon (6 g) salt
- 1 cup (100 g) olives, whole and pitted
- 3½ ounces (100 g) feta cheese, crumbled

1. In a large bowl, combine the recipe starter with the warm water and mix gently.

2. In another bowl, combine the two flours and the salt.

3. Add the flour mix to the first bowl and mix using one hand until a dough forms. This takes only a couple of minutes. It's a good idea to use only one hand, leaving the other one clean for using utensils, etc. Use a plastic dough scraper around the bowl to make sure all the flour is mixed in. Cover the bowl with a shower cap or damp dish towel and let it rest.

4. After 5 to 10 minutes, give the dough a fold in the bowl. Use slightly wet hands to prevent the dough sticking to them. Pull a section of the dough out to the side and fold it into the middle of the ball. Repeat this going around the ball of dough until you get back to the beginning (four or five folds). Use the scraper to turn the dough upside down, cover the bowl, and leave for another 5 to 10 minutes. Repeat this three times.

   After the final fold, cover the bowl again and let rest for 1 hour.

5. Turn the dough out of the bowl onto a lightly floured counter. Stretch out one side of the dough and fold it into the middle. Repeat this with each of the four "sides" of the dough. Put the dough back in the bowl upside down and let rest for another hour.

6. **Shaping a loaf in a pan:** Lightly grease a 2-pound loaf pan. Turn the dough out onto a well-floured counter and spread it out into a narrow rectangle. Spread the olives and feta evenly across it. Take the narrow end of the rectangle and roll it into a very tight cylinder.

7. Place the dough in the pan with one open end of the cylinder facing upward, so you can see a spiral of the olives and feta.

8. Follow the rest of the Basic Sourdough recipe from Step 8 (page 47) to the end, baking the loaf in the pan, not on the baking sheet, and baking for an additional 10 minutes. Remove the bread from the pan to check if it is baked through and to cool.

MAKES 1 loaf **EQUIPMENT** 2-pound loaf pan

SWEET POTATO AND ROSEMARY SOURDOUGH

MAKES 1 loaf **EQUIPMENT** oval proofing basket **DF V+**

≡

If you like your bread a little lighter, the extra starch in sweet potato flour gives the dough a spring and a softer texture not generally associated with a traditional sourdough. In fact, adding a potato to a bake to bulk it out was common practice in times when grain was expensive. We prefer to use sweet potato because it is high in fiber, vitamin C, manganese, potassium, and thiamin—and its lovely, rich color—but either works well. The hint of rosemary, always great with a potato recipe, makes this bread good with a veg soup and as a base for a tartine—try goat cheese and caramelized red onion.

DAY 1

- 8½ tablespoons (75 g) white bread flour
- 5 tablespoons (75 g) warm water (90 to 99°F)
- Active Wheat Starter (page 41)

Mix the flour and water with the whole quantity of the starter and leave loosely covered at room temperature overnight.

- 1 large sweet potato (about 8 ounces/225 g)

Bake the sweet potato in its skin for 30 to 40 minutes until soft. Mash coarsely with a fork and let cool overnight.

DAY 2

- 5½ ounces (150 g) recipe starter from Day 1
- 1 cup (225 g) warm water (90 to 99°F)
- Roasted, mashed sweet potato from Day 1
- 3⅓ cups (500 g) white bread flour
- 1 teaspoon (5 g) rosemary, minced
- 1½ teaspoons (8 g) salt

1. In a large bowl, combine the recipe starter with the warm water and sweet potato. Mix gently.

2. In another bowl, combine the flour, rosemary, and the salt.

3. Add the flour mix to the first bowl and mix using one hand until a dough forms. This takes only a couple of minutes. It's a good idea to use only one hand, leaving the other one clean for using utensils, etc. Use a plastic dough scraper around the bowl to make sure all the flour is mixed in. Cover the bowl with a shower cap or damp dish towel and let it rest.

4. After 5 to 10 minutes, give the dough a fold in the bowl. Use slightly wet hands to prevent the dough sticking to them. Pull a section of the dough out to the side and fold it into the middle of the ball. Repeat this going around the ball of dough until you get back to the beginning (four or five folds). Use the scraper to turn the dough upside down, cover the bowl, and leave for another 5 to 10 minutes. Repeat this three times. After the final fold, cover the bowl and let rest for 1 hour.

5. Turn the dough out of the bowl onto a lightly floured counter. Stretch out one side of the dough and fold it into the middle. Repeat this with each of the four "sides" of the dough. Put the dough back in the bowl upside down and let rest for another hour.

6. Follow the rest of the Basic Sourdough recipe from Step 6 (page 46) to the end.

BROCCOLI AND STICHELTON SOURDOUGH

≡

Lindsay trained as a baker at the School of Artisan Food on the Welbeck Estate in Nottinghamshire, UK, which is also the home of Stichelton, a blue cheese based on stilton but made with raw milk. So when it came to choosing a cheese to pair with broccoli for a weekend special sourdough, Stichelton seemed an obvious choice. It has a more complex flavor than stilton and creates delicious pockets of gooey, salty cheesiness in the bread. But if you can't get hold of it, stilton or any other good-quality blue cheese will work as well. This loaf is guaranteed to polarize any audience, especially a young one, but like all these savory breads, served with a buffet lunch or as a tartine base or accompanying a homemade soup they perform a job beyond that of a regular loaf. And let's face it, with bread being such a staple, ringing the changes from time to time enlivens the senses, and this one does that especially well.

DAY 1

- 6 tablespoons (50 g) white bread flour
- 3½ tablespoons (50 g) warm water (90 to 99°F)
- Active Wheat Starter (page 41)

Mix the flour and water with the whole quantity of the starter and leave loosely covered at room temperature overnight.

DAY 2

- 3½ ounces (100 g) recipe starter from Day 1
- Generous 1 cup (270 g) warm water (90 to 99°F)
- 2⅓ cups (335 g) white bread flour
- ⅓ cup (40 g) light rye flour
- 1½ teaspoons (8 g) salt
- 3½ ounces (100 g) raw broccoli, cut into small florets
- 3½ ounces (100 g) Stichelton, crumbled into small chunks

MAKES 1 loaf **EQUIPMENT** round proofing basket

1 In a large bowl, combine the recipe starter with the warm water and mix gently.

2 In another bowl, combine the two flours and the salt.

3 Add the flour mix to the first bowl and mix using one hand until a dough forms. This takes only a couple of minutes. It's a good idea to use only one hand, leaving the other one clean for using utensils, etc. Use a plastic dough scraper around the bowl to make sure all the flour is mixed in. Cover the bowl with a shower cap or damp dish towel and let it rest.

4 After 5 to 10 minutes, give the dough a fold in the bowl. Use slightly wet hands to prevent the dough sticking to them. Pull a section of the dough out to the side and fold it into the middle of the ball. Repeat this going around the ball of dough until you get back to the beginning (four or five folds). Use the scraper to turn the dough upside down, cover the bowl, and leave for another 5 to 10 minutes. Repeat this another two times.

Add the broccoli and cheese to the dough and fold for a third and final time, making sure the cheese and broccoli are evenly distributed. Don't worry if they start to break down slightly as you mix; this actually makes for a nicer final result.

After the final fold, cover the bowl again and let rest for 1 hour.

5 Turn the dough out of the bowl onto a lightly floured counter. Stretch out one side of the dough and fold it into the middle. Repeat this with each of the four "sides" of the dough. Put the dough back in the bowl upside down and let rest for another hour.

6 **Shaping a round loaf:** Once the dough has rested, turn it out onto a lightly floured counter. To shape the dough, stretch one side out and fold it into the middle. Repeat this all around the outside of the dough until you get back to your starting point. Flip it so the seam side is down. Use your left hand to hold the dough in place and use your right hand to rotate the dough, tucking it under and tightening it as you go around (if you are left-handed you might want to use your right hand to stabilize and your left hand to rotate). The idea here is to increase the strength of the dough without tearing it. The final surface of the dough should be taut to the touch.

7 Lightly flour a round proofing basket and place the dough in it, seam side up.

8 Follow the rest of the Basic Sourdough recipe from Step 8 (page 47) to the end, but bake for an additional 5 minutes.

BEET AND SAUERKRAUT SOURDOUGH

MAKES 1 loaf **EQUIPMENT** high-speed blender and oval proofing basket **DF** **V+**

This loaf is a showstopper. We created it for our first collaboration with Soho House, a pop-up five-course menu of fermented foods, and served it with our own home-cultured butter. We knew we wanted a sauerkraut bread, but the idea to combine it with beet came from Lindsay.

Pureed beet replaces the water and gives the loaf a vibrant dark pink color. The sauerkraut tang works wonderfully with the earthiness of the beet and the texture is simply beguiling. Drain the sauerkraut well, or the dough will be too slack and the acidity of the juice could affect the gluten development.

DAY 1

- 8½ tablespoons (75 g) white bread flour
- 5 tablespoons (75 g) warm water (90 to 99°F)
- Active Wheat Starter (page 41)

Mix the flour and water with the whole quantity of the starter and leave loosely covered at room temperature overnight.

DAY 2

- 5½ ounces (150 g) recipe starter from Day 1
- 12 ounces (350 g) raw beet, peeled and pureed
- 3¼ cups (350 g) white bread flour
- 1½ teaspoons (8 g) Himalayan pink salt
- 3½ ounces (100 g) raw sauerkraut, drained of as much liquid as possible

NUTRITION NOTE

Sauerkraut is fermented cabbage and is fantastically good for you, but do ensure you use a good-quality one, or preferably make your own. It should be fresh, from the chiller cabinet, and raw. The only ingredients should be cabbage and salt.

1. In a large bowl, combine the recipe starter with the beet puree and mix gently.

2. In another bowl, combine the flour and the salt.

3. Add the flour mix to the first bowl and mix using one hand until a dough forms. This takes only a couple of minutes. It's a good idea to use only one hand, leaving the other one clean for using utensils, etc. Use a plastic dough scraper around the bowl to make sure all the flour is mixed in. Cover the bowl with a shower cap or damp dish towel and let it rest.

4. After 5 to 10 minutes, give the dough a fold in the bowl. Use slightly wet hands to prevent the dough sticking to them. Pull a section of the dough out to the side and fold it into the middle of the ball. Repeat this going around the ball of dough until you get back to the beginning (four or five folds). Use the scraper to turn the dough upside down, cover the bowl, and leave for another 5 to 10 minutes. Repeat this two times.

   For the third and final fold, add the drained sauerkraut to the dough and fold well so that it is evenly distributed throughout. After the final fold, cover the bowl again and let rest for 1 hour.

5. Turn the dough out of the bowl onto a lightly floured counter. Stretch out one side of the dough and fold it into the middle. Repeat this with each of the four "sides" of the dough. Put the dough back in the bowl upside down and let rest for another hour.

6. Follow the rest of the Basic Sourdough recipe from Step 6 (page 46) to the end, but bake for an additional 10 minutes.

SEAWEED PESTO TEAR AND SHARE SOURDOUGH

Slicing bread can sometimes feel a bit of a chore, especially if you're picnicking or want your bread to look a bit more rustic at the table. This loaf is fantastic because it just tears apart. It's almost as if you cut the slices before you even bake it. This isn't as labor intensive as it sounds, it's actually a very easy loaf to shape, and anyway the quality of the shaping is much less important than for a "normal" loaf.

Pesto flavors work well with doughs, though too much can become overpowering. Homemade is always best, of course. We add a touch of seaweed, mainly for its diverse nutrition (few on a Western diet consume enough iodine), but also for its subtle flavors that give even more depth. Enjoy this fab bread dipped in olive oil and with pickled condiments.

DAY 1

- ½ cup (60 g) white bread flour
- ¼ cup (60 g) warm water (90 to 99°F)
- Active Wheat Starter (page 41)

Mix the flour and water with the whole quantity of the starter and leave loosely covered at room temperature overnight.

DAY 2

- 4¼ ounces (120 g) recipe starter from Day 1
- 1⅓ cups (320 g) warm water (90 to 99°F)
- 3¼ cups (440 g) white bread flour
- 1½ teaspoons (8 g) salt
- 2 tablespoons (25 g) extra virgin olive oil

FOR THE PESTO

- ¼ cup (30 g) walnuts
- 2 garlic cloves, peeled
- 3⅓ cups (80 g) fresh basil leaves
- ¼ cup (60 g) extra virgin olive oil
- 1 teaspoon (5 g) lemon juice
- ½ teaspoon (2.5 g) kombu seaweed flakes

MAKES 1 loaf **EQUIPMENT** food processor and 2-pound loaf pan **DF V+**

1. In a large bowl, combine the recipe starter with the warm water and mix gently.
2. In another bowl, combine the flour and the salt.
3. Add the flour mix to the first bowl and mix using one hand until a dough forms. This takes only a couple of minutes. It's a good idea to use only one hand, leaving the other one clean for using utensils, etc. Use a plastic dough scraper around the bowl to make sure all the flour is mixed in. Cover the bowl with a shower cap or damp dish towel and let it rest.
4. After 5 to 10 minutes, give the dough a fold in the bowl. Use slightly wet hands to prevent the dough sticking to them. Pull a section of the dough out to the side and fold it into the middle of the ball. Repeat this going around the ball of dough until you get back to the beginning (four or five folds). Use the scraper to turn the dough upside down, cover the bowl, and leave for another 5 to 10 minutes. Repeat this another two times. For the third and final fold, add the olive oil to the dough and fold well so that it is completely combined. If you add the oil earlier it can prevent the gluten from developing. After the final fold, cover the bowl and let rest for 1 hour.
5. After the hour, turn the dough out of the bowl and place on a lightly floured counter. Stretch one side of the dough out and fold into the middle. Repeat this with each of the four "corners" of the dough. Place upside down in the bowl again and let rest for another hour.
6. To make the pesto, place the walnuts and garlic in a food processor and whizz until finely chopped. Add the basil, oil, lemon juice, and seaweed and pulse a few more times.
7. **Shaping a tear and share loaf:** Lightly grease a 2-pound loaf pan. Turn out the dough onto a lightly floured counter. Roll it out to 16 × 12 inches. Cut the dough into twelve 4-inch squares. Spread all but one of the squares with the pesto. Stack the dough squares on top of each other with the pesto side up. Finish with the plain square, so that each end of the pile is free from pesto.
8. Carefully turn the stack onto its side and lift it into the pan. The top can be quite rough as this will give a nice texture to the loaf.
9. Follow the rest of the Basic Sourdough recipe from Step 8 (page 47) to the end, baking the loaf in the pan, not on the baking sheet. Remove the bread from the pan to check if it is baked through and to cool.

GREEN TEA, LEMON, AND GOLDEN RAISIN SOURDOUGH

MAKES 1 loaf
EQUIPMENT 2-pound loaf pan
DF V+

☰

This loaf is inspired by drinking lemon in green tea at the start of the day to get the body moving. It's a delicious breakfast bread; it will perk you up straightaway.

We soak the golden raisins overnight in the tea and lemon zest. This stops them taking moisture from the final dough, which would dry it out and make a less consistent loaf. It also allows the golden raisins to soak up a lot of the liquid's flavors.

This loaf is really easy to adapt to your tastes. We've made a few suggestions at the end.

DAY 1

- 8½ tablespoons (75 g) white bread flour
- 5 tablespoons (75 g) warm water (90 to 99°F)
- Active Wheat Starter (page 41)

Mix the flour and water with the whole quantity of the starter and leave loosely covered at room temperature overnight.

- ½ cup (120 g) hot water (doesn't have to be boiling)
- ¾ cup (120 g) golden raisins
- Zest of 1 lemon, grated
- 2 green tea bags

In a bowl, combine the hot water, golden raisins, lemon zest, and tea bags. Let soak overnight at room temperature.

DAY 2

- Tea and fruit mix from Day 1
- 5½ ounces (150 g) recipe starter from Day 1
- Scant 1 cup (190 g) warm water (90 to 99°F)
- Generous 2 cups (300 g) white bread flour
- 6 tablespoons (50 g) sprouted whole wheat flour
- 1½ teaspoons (8 g) salt

1 Remove the tea bags from the fruit mix and discard. Drain the liquid from the golden raisins and set it aside.

2 In a large bowl, combine the recipe starter with the warm water and mix gently. To this add the reserved tea from the fruit and mix gently.

3 In another bowl, combine the two flours and the salt.

4 Add the flour mix to the first bowl and mix using one hand until a dough forms. This takes only a couple of minutes. It's a good idea to use only one hand, leaving the other one clean for using utensils, etc. Use a plastic dough scraper around the bowl to make sure all the flour is mixed in. Cover the bowl with a shower cap or damp dish towel and let it rest.

5 After 5 to 10 minutes, give the dough a fold in the bowl. Use slightly wet hands to prevent the dough sticking to them. Pull a section of the dough out to the side and fold it into the middle of the ball. Repeat this going around the ball of dough until you get back to the beginning (four or five folds). Use the scraper to turn the dough upside down, cover the bowl, and leave for another 5 to 10 minutes. Repeat this another two times.

For the third and final fold, add the golden

raisins. We add them at this stage so that they don't interrupt the development of the gluten. Fold until the golden raisins are distributed evenly throughout the dough. After the final fold, cover the bowl again and let rest for 1 hour.

6 Turn the dough out onto a lightly floured counter. Stretch out one side of the dough and fold it into the middle. Repeat this with each of the four "sides" of the dough. Put the dough back in the bowl upside down and let rest for another hour.

7 **Shaping a loaf in a pan:** Lightly grease a 2-pound loaf pan. Turn the dough out onto a floured counter. Stretch it so that the dough is in a long, flattened oval shape. Fold each end of the dough into the middle, so the dough forms a rectangle with a vertical seam down the middle. Now pull and fold the top of the rectangle in toward you, so that it covers a third of the way down. Tuck the dough in with your thumbs. Repeat this until you have a sausage shape. Roll it to tighten it slightly and make the shape as even as possible.

8 Place the dough in the pan, seam side down.

9 Follow the rest of the Basic Sourdough recipe from Step 8 (page 47) to the end, baking the loaf in the pan, not on the baking sheet, and baking for an additional 10 minutes. Remove the bread from the pan to check if it is baked through and to cool.

VARIATIONS

CHAI TEA, ORANGE, AND CRANBERRY SOURDOUGH

For Christmas we like to make a variation of this with chai tea instead of green tea, scant 1 cup (100 g) cranberries instead of golden raisins, and orange zest instead of lemon.

EARL GREY TEA AND PEACH SOURDOUGH

Another great variation replaces the cranberries with chopped dried peaches and the green tea with black tea—we particularly like Earl Grey.

SPROUTED WHOLE WHEAT SOURDOUGH

≡

Sprouted grains are nutritional powerhouses. You sprout grains by soaking them in water, which makes them start to grow, releasing vital nutrients. In addition, the resulting enzyme activity transforms the nutrients, making them easier for the body to absorb. If you cannot find sprouted whole wheat flour, you can use this recipe to make a standard whole wheat sourdough. You will still get the benefit of the additional bran in the flour, but without quite so many accessible nutrients.

To all the world this looks like a classic whole wheat loaf and its flavor, albeit with a sourdough twist, is that pure distinctive whole wheat taste we all grew up with.

DAY 1

- ⅔ cup (80 g) light rye flour
- ⅓ cup (80 g) warm water (90 to 99°F)
- Active Wheat Starter (page 41)

Mix the flour and water with the whole quantity of the starter and leave loosely covered at room temperature overnight.

DAY 2

- 3½ ounces (100 g) recipe starter from Day 1
- 1¼ cups (305 g) warm water (90 to 99°F)
- 3¼ cups (460 g) sprouted whole wheat flour
- 1½ teaspoons (8 g) salt

NUTRITION NOTE

The benefits of sprouted grains are being investigated by nutritionists everywhere as a breakthrough ingredient. It's always fun to try to keep up with these kinds of developments.

MAKES 1 loaf **EQUIPMENT** 2-pound loaf pan **DF V+**

1. In a large bowl, combine the recipe starter with the warm water and mix gently.

2. In another bowl, combine the flour and the salt. Always mix the salt into the flour, as salt will kill the active agents, the bacteria and yeast, if it comes into direct contact with them.

3. Add the flour mix to the first bowl and mix using one hand until a dough forms. This takes only a couple of minutes. It's a good idea to use only one hand, leaving the other one clean for using utensils, etc. Use a plastic dough scraper around the bowl to make sure all the flour is mixed in. Cover the bowl with a shower cap or damp dish towel and let it rest.

4. After 5 to 10 minutes, give the dough a fold in the bowl. Use slightly wet hands to prevent the dough sticking to them. Pull a section of the dough out to the side and fold it into the middle of the ball. Repeat this going around the ball of dough until you get back to the beginning (four or five folds). Use the scraper to turn the dough upside down, cover the bowl, and leave for another 5 to 10 minutes. Repeat this three times.

   After the final fold, cover the bowl again and let it rest for 1 hour.

5. Turn the dough out of the bowl onto a lightly floured counter. Stretch out one side of the dough and fold it into the middle. Repeat this with each of the four "sides" of the dough. Put the dough back in the bowl upside down and let rest for another hour.

6. **Shaping a loaf in a pan:** Once the dough has rested, it's time to shape it, using both hands. Turn it out onto a lightly floured counter and stretch it out into a long, flattened oval shape. Take one end of the dough and fold it into the middle. Repeat with the other end, so that the dough now resembles a rectangle. The two ends should overlap a little in the middle. Pull and fold the top of the rectangle in toward you so that it covers a third of the way down. Tuck the dough in with your thumbs. Repeat this until you get a sausage shape. Roll it to tighten it slightly and make the shape as even as possible.

7. Lightly grease a 2-pound loaf pan. Place the dough in the pan so that the seam is facing down.

8. Follow the rest of the Basic Sourdough recipe from Step 8 (page 47) to the end, baking the loaf in the pan, not on the baking sheet. Remove the bread from the pan to check if it is baked through and to cool.

APPLE AND CIDER SOURDOUGH

MAKES 1 loaf **EQUIPMENT** round proofing basket **DF V+**

≡

This is a loaf that Lindsay was developing at the point I met her. It's the one she baked to persuade me that she was the right person for the job. It told me all I needed to know about Lindsay's lively imagination as well as her technical ability—exactly the blend I was after. The hint of vinegar from the cider goes so well with the sourdough, and the loaf has a lovely fall aroma. It's delicious toasted (peanut butter makes a particularly good topping) or as a cheese sandwich.

DAY 1

- 8½ tablespoons (75 g) white bread flour
- 5 tablespoons (75 g) warm water (90 to 99°F)
- Active Wheat Starter (page 41)

Mix the flour and water with the whole quantity of the starter and leave loosely covered at room temperature overnight.

- 4¼ ounces (120 g) dried apple, chopped into small pieces
- ½ cup (120 g) organic cider

Soak the chopped dried apple in the cider overnight. By soaking the fruit you add to its flavor and prevent it taking moisture from the dough, which would result in a drier loaf.

DAY 2

- 5½ ounces (150 g) recipe starter from Day 1
- Scant 1 cup (190 g) warm water (90 to 99°F)
- ½ cup (120 g) organic cider
- 2½ cups (350 g) white bread flour
- 1½ teaspoons (8 g) salt

1. Drain the cider from the apples and set it aside.

2. In a large bowl, combine the recipe starter with the water and the cider and mix gently.

3. In another bowl, combine the flour and the salt.

4. Add the flour mix to the first bowl and mix using one hand until a dough forms. This takes only a couple of minutes. It's a good idea to use only one hand, leaving the other one clean for using utensils, etc. Use a plastic dough scraper around the bowl to make sure all the flour is mixed in. Cover the bowl with a shower cap or damp dish towel and let it rest.

5. After 5 to 10 minutes, give the dough a fold in the bowl. Use slightly wet hands to prevent the dough sticking to them. Pull a section of the dough out to the side and fold it into the middle of the ball. Repeat this going around the ball of dough until you get back to the beginning (four or five folds). Use the scraper to turn the dough upside down, cover the bowl, and leave for another 5 to 10 minutes. Repeat this two times. For the third and final fold, add the apple pieces and fold until they are distributed evenly throughout the dough. After the final fold, cover the bowl again and let rest for 1 hour.

6. Turn the dough out of the bowl onto a lightly floured counter. Stretch out one side of the dough and fold it into the middle. Repeat this with each of the four "sides" of the dough. Put the dough back in the bowl upside down and let rest for another hour.

7. **Shaping a round loaf:** Once the dough has rested, turn it out onto a lightly floured

counter. Stretch one side of the dough out and fold it into the middle. Repeat this all around the outside of the dough until you get back to your starting point. Flip it so the seam side is facing down. Use your left hand to hold the dough in place and use your right hand to rotate the dough, tucking it under and tightening it as you go around (if you are left-handed you might want to use your right hand to stabilize and your left hand to rotate). The idea here is to increase the strength of the dough without tearing it. The final surface of the dough should be taut to the touch.

8 Lightly flour a round proofing basket and place the dough in it, seam facing up.

9 Follow the rest of the Basic Sourdough recipe from Step 8 (page 47) to the end, but bake for an additional 5 minutes. For this loaf we like to use a circle slash on the top, so that it almost looks like an apple popping out of the loaf. This is quite a dark bread, and you will have to keep an eye on it to make sure that any apple on the outside doesn't burn too much.

SUPERLOAF WITH CHIA AND QUINOA

MAKES 1 loaf
EQUIPMENT round proofing basket
DF V+

≡

We invented this loaf because we wanted one that provided good-quality protein (from the quinoa) and omega-3s and healthy fats (from the chia). It's the perfect slice for the sourdough avocado-on-toast combo, so universally fashionable all of a sudden.

We put a distinctive cross on the top, which gives this loaf a bit of swagger, and when sliced the distinctive black dots of the chia seeds makes this look and feel very contemporary.

DAY 1

- ¾ cup (100 g) white bread flour
- 7 tablespoons (100 g) warm water (90 to 99°F)
- Active Wheat Starter (page 41)

Mix the flour and water with the whole quantity of the starter and leave loosely covered at room temperature overnight.

DAY 2

- 7 ounces (200 g) recipe starter from Day 1
- 1 cup (225 g) warm water (90 to 99°F)
- 1⅓ cups (195 g) white bread flour
- 1 cup (145 g) sprouted whole wheat or kamut flour
- 1½ teaspoons (8 g) salt
- Scant 1 cup (175 g) cooked and cooled quinoa
- 1 tablespoon (15 g) chia seeds

1. In a large bowl, combine the recipe starter and warm water and mix gently.

2. In another bowl, combine the two flours and the salt.

3. Add the flour mix to the first bowl and mix using one hand until a dough forms. This takes only a couple of minutes. It's a good idea to use only one hand, leaving the other one clean for using utensils, etc. Use a plastic dough scraper around the bowl to make sure all the flour is mixed in. Cover the bowl with a shower cap or damp dish towel and let it rest.

4. After 5 to 10 minutes, give the dough a fold in the bowl. Use slightly wet hands to prevent the dough sticking to them. Pull a section of the dough out to the side and fold it into the middle of the ball. Repeat this going around the ball of dough until you get back to the beginning (four or five folds). Use the scraper to turn the dough upside down, cover the bowl, and leave for another 5 to 10 minutes. Repeat this another two times, then for the third and final fold, add the cooked quinoa and chia seeds and fold enough to make sure that they are spread evenly through the dough.

   After the final fold, cover the bowl again and let it rest for 1 hour.

5. Turn the dough out of the bowl onto a lightly floured counter. Stretch out one side of the dough and fold it into the middle. Repeat this with each of the four "sides" of the dough. Put the dough back in the bowl upside down and let rest for another hour.

6 **Shaping a round loaf:** Once the dough has rested, turn it out onto a lightly floured counter. Stretch one side of the dough out and fold it into the middle. Repeat this all around the outside of the dough until you get back to your starting point. Flip it so the seam side is facing down. Use your left hand to hold the dough in place and use your right hand to rotate the dough, tucking it under and tightening it as you go around (if you are left-handed you might want to use your right hand to stabilize and your left hand to rotate). The idea here is to increase the strength of the dough without tearing it. The final surface of the dough should be taut to the touch.

7 Lightly flour the round proofing basket and place the dough in it with the seam facing up and the smooth side on the bottom. We use unlined baskets as they give an attractive pattern on the final loaf.

8 Follow the rest of the Basic Sourdough recipe from Step 8 (page 47) to the end, but bake for an additional 5 minutes.

SOURDOUGH FOCACCIA

≡

Being a halfway house between pizza and bread, focaccia deserves mastering, as indeed it is throughout Italy, where there are seemingly no limits to its flavor variations. We rarely bake it in the store because space restricts our lunch-based offerings, but as we expand it will definitely feature. The extra flavor the sourdough brings is very noticeable, not to mention the improved nutrition that comes with it too! Like pizza, focaccia is very adaptable, so feel free to play around with ingredients, whatever catches your imagination. It's a perfect centerpiece to a simple meal.

DAY 1

- 6 tablespoons (50 g) wheat flour
- 7 tablespoons (100 g) warm water (90 to 99°F)
- Active Wheat Starter (page 41)

Mix the flour and water with the whole quantity of the starter and leave loosely covered at room temperature overnight.

DAY 2

- 3½ ounces (100 g) recipe starter from Day 1
- Generous 1 cup (250 g) warm water (90 to 99°F)
- 2⅓ cups (330 g) white bread flour
- 1 teaspoon (6 g) salt
- Generous ¼ cup (70 g) extra virgin olive oil

FOR THE TOPPINGS

- 1 teaspoon coarse Himalayan pink salt
- Handful of fresh rosemary
- Drizzle of extra virgin olive oil

1. In a large bowl, combine the recipe starter with the warm water and mix gently.

2. In another bowl, combine the flour and the salt.

3. Add the flour mixture to the first bowl and mix using one hand until a dough forms. This takes only a couple of minutes. It's a good idea to use only one hand, leaving the other one clean for using utensils, etc. Use a plastic dough scraper around the bowl to make sure all the flour is mixed in. Pour the olive oil over the top of the dough and let stand for 20 minutes at room temperature. The oil will prevent it drying out.

MAKES 1 loaf **EQUIPMENT** 8-inch round cake pan **DF V+**

4 After 20 minutes fold the dough in the bowl, incorporating some of the olive oil as you do so. Pull a section of the dough out to the side and fold it into the middle of the ball. Repeat this going around the ball of dough until you get back to the beginning (four or five folds). At this stage you do not need to worry about incorporating all the oil. Let the dough stand for another 20 minutes, then repeat the process four more times.

   After the final fold, let it rest for 1 hour.

5 Turn the dough into a greased 8-inch round cake pan and let it stand at room temperature for 2 to 3 hours, covered with a shower cap or damp dish towel, until the dough is looking lively and there are plenty of large bubbles forming.

6 Preheat the oven to 425°F.

7 Top the focaccia dough with a sprinkling of salt, some fresh rosemary, and another drizzle of olive oil. Now press into the dough all over with your fingertips.

8 Bake for 30 minutes until golden, then turn out onto a wire rack to cool and drizzle with some more olive oil while it's still warm.

VARIATIONS

CRÈME FRAÎCHE AND ONION

- 3 tablespoons (45 g) crème fraîche
- 1 onion, finely sliced
- ½ teaspoon (2.5 g) dried oregano

Before baking, spread the crème fraîche on top of the focaccia, sprinkle over the onions evenly, and sprinkle with the dried oregano.

BLACK OLIVE AND LEMON

- Handful of black olives, pitted and halved
- Zest of 1 lemon, finely grated

Before baking, sprinkle the olives over the focaccia. As soon as it comes out of the oven, sprinkle with the lemon zest.

CHERRY TOMATO, BASIL, AND AVOCADO OIL

- Avocado oil
- Handful of cherry tomatoes, halved
- Handful of fresh basil leaves, torn

Replace the olive oil in the recipe with avocado oil. Avocado oil has a mild fragrance, a creamy texture, and a rich, lingering taste that's both naturally buttery and slightly nutty. Avocado oil can support everything from good cardiovascular function to healthy aging. Before baking, sprinkle the cherry tomatoes over the focaccia. As soon as it comes out of the oven, toss some torn basil leaves over the top and drizzle with some more avocado oil.

CHOCOLATE, HAZELNUT, AND RAISIN SPELT SOURDOUGH

≡

This is probably our most indulgent loaf, and one of our sweeter sourdoughs. It goes down an absolute treat with customers and children often refer to it as the "Nutella" loaf.

It is delicious on its own, or toast it and top with yogurt and fresh berries. The flavors in a sourdough spelt always fuse really well with chocolate, and of course chocolate always works well with hazelnuts.

DAY 1

- ⅓ cup (80 g) warm water (90 to 99°F)
- ¾ cup (80 g) light rye flour
- Active Wheat Starter (page 41)

Add the water and rye flour to the whole quantity of the starter and leave loosely covered overnight at room temperature.

DAY 2

- 5¾ ounces (160 g) recipe starter from Day 1
- Scant 1 cup (200 g) warm water (90 to 99°F)
- 2½ cups (330 g) white spelt flour
- ⅓ cup (30 g) raw cacao powder
- 1 teaspoon (6 g) salt
- Scant ½ cup (80 g) coconut sugar
- Sweetened chocolate chips or chop up some of your favorite healthy chocolate
- 1 cup (150 g) raisins
- Scant 1 cup (110 g) hazelnuts

MAKES 1 loaf **EQUIPMENT** 2-pound loaf pan **DF V+**

1 In a large bowl, combine the recipe starter and water and mix gently.

2 In another bowl, combine the flour, cacao, salt, and sugar. Always mix the salt with the flour as salt will kill the starter if it comes into direct contact with it.

3 Add the flour mix to the first bowl and combine with your hands until a dough forms. Use the dough scraper around the bowl to make sure that all the flour is incorporated. Cover the bowl with a shower cap or a damp dish towel and let it rest.

4 After 5 to 10 minutes, give the dough a fold in the bowl. Use slightly wet hands to prevent the dough sticking to them. Pull a section of the dough out to the side and fold it into the middle of the ball. Repeat this going around the ball of dough until you get back to the beginning (four or five folds). Use the scraper to turn the dough upside down, cover the bowl, and leave for another 5 to 10 minutes. Repeat this another two times. For the third and final fold, add the chocolate chips, raisins, and hazelnuts and fold enough to make sure they are spread evenly through the dough. After the final fold, cover the bowl again and let it rest for 1 hour.

5 Turn the dough out of the bowl onto a lightly floured counter. Stretch out one side of the dough and fold it into the middle. Repeat this with each of the four "sides" of the dough. Put the dough back in the bowl upside down and let rest for another hour.

6 **Shaping a loaf in a pan:** Once the dough has rested, it's time to shape it, using both hands. Turn it out onto a lightly floured counter and stretch it out into a long, flattened oval shape. Take one end of the dough and fold it into the middle. Repeat with the other end, so that the dough now resembles a rectangle. The two ends should overlap a little in the middle. Pull and fold the top of the rectangle in toward you so that it covers a third of the way down. Tuck the dough in with your thumbs. Repeat this until you get a sausage shape. Roll it to tighten it slightly and make the shape as even as possible.

7 Lightly grease a 2-pound loaf pan. Place the dough in the pan with the seam side down.

8 Follow the rest of the Basic Sourdough recipe from Step 8 (page 47) to the end, baking the loaf in the pan, not on the baking sheet. Remove the bread from the pan to check if it is baked through and to cool.

RYE SOURDOUGH

≡

Rye is pretty much synonymous with northeast Europe, where it flourishes in the inhospitable places where wheat refuses to grow. The resultant rye flour acts very differently from wheat flour.

It's important to let the baked rye loaf rest for around 24 hours before you eat it. In this time the crumb becomes firm and more stable, which makes it easier to digest. The flavor develops even more, too. If you eat it too soon it can cause problems for your digestion. So this really is a perfect embodiment of "slow" food, where not taking shortcuts pays handsome dividends.

The distinctive flavor of rye bread can be quite a shock to any palate used to wheat bread, but it's a delicious loaf that pairs incredibly well with many different flavors—smoked salmon, hard cheese, apples, berries, honey—and the list goes on.

DAY 1

- Scant 1½ cups (170 g) light rye flour
- ¾ cup (170 g) warm water (90 to 99°F)
- Active Rye Starter (page 42)

Mix the flour and water with the whole quantity of the starter and leave loosely covered at room temperature overnight.

DAY 2

- 12 ounces (340 g) recipe starter from Day 1
- 1 cup (245 g) warm water (90 to 99°F)
- Generous 2¾ cups (340 g) light rye flour
- 1½ teaspoons (8 g) salt

MAKES 1 loaf **EQUIPMENT** 2-pound loaf pan **DF** **V+**

1. In a large bowl, combine the recipe starter with the warm water and mix gently.

2. In another bowl, combine the flour and the salt. Always mix the salt into the flour, as salt will kill the active agents, the bacteria and yeast, if it comes into direct contact with them.

3. Add the flour and salt mix to the first bowl. Stir well with your hands or a wooden spoon until thoroughly combined. It will be more like a batter than a dough, so kneading won't develop the gluten.

4. Lightly grease a 2-pound loaf pan.

5. Pour the mixture into the pan and smooth over the top. Dust with a little more rye flour.

6. Leave the pan at room temperature for 3 to 4 hours, or until the mix more or less reaches the top of the pan.

7. Preheat the oven to 500°F. Place a roasting pan in the bottom of the oven to heat up. Fill a cup with water and place to one side ready to use.

8. Place the pan in the oven and pour the glass of water into the roasting pan.

9. Turn the temperature down to 475°F and bake for 45 minutes. To check that the loaf is baked through, turn it out of the pan and tap the bottom—it should sound hollow. If not, return it to the oven for another 5 to 10 minutes.

10. Once baked, turn the loaf out onto a wire rack. Let cool for 24 hours before eating.

RYE SEEDED SOURDOUGH

MAKES 1 loaf **EQUIPMENT** 2-pound loaf pan **DF V+**

≡

Our customers always seem to be drawn to our seeded loaves, and the rye seeded is no exception. This is one of our most Instagrammed breads! It's often shown topped with avocado, scrambled egg, or a big fresh tomato and basil salad, and all other manner of things. It's such a good base for any meal because of the depth of flavor that the rye brings. It feels somehow more than just a slice of bread.

NUTRITION NOTE

Among common cereals, the dietary fiber content of whole grain rye is the highest, with over three times that of standard white bread. And when rye is combined with a mixture of seeds, which too are high in fiber, it becomes a great food for your gut health.

DAY 1

- Scant 1 cup (110 g) light rye flour
- ½ cup (110 g) warm water (90 to 99°F)
- Active Rye Starter (page 42)

Mix the flour and warm water with the whole quantity of the starter and leave loosely covered at room temperature overnight.

DAY 2

- 7¾ ounces (220 g) recipe starter from Day 1
- ⅔ cup (160 g) water (90 to 99°F)
- Scant 2 cups (220 g) light rye flour
- 1½ teaspoons (8 g) salt
- ¾ cup (100 g) mixed seeds (we like to use a mix of pumpkin, sunflower, sesame, and flaxseed)
- Extra mixed seeds, for topping

1. In a large bowl, combine the recipe starter with the warm water and mix gently.

2. In another bowl, combine the flour, salt, and seeds. Always mix the salt into the flour, as salt will kill the active agents, the bacteria and yeast, if it comes into direct contact with them.

3. Add the flour, salt, and seeds mix to the first bowl. Stir well with your hands or a wooden spoon until thoroughly combined. It will be more like a batter than a dough, so kneading won't develop the gluten.

4. Lightly grease a 2-pound loaf pan.

5. Pour the mixture into the pan and smooth over the top. Sprinkle with more seeds.

6. Follow the rest of the Rye Sourdough recipe from Step 6 (page 81) to the end.

WHOLE GRAIN RYE AND BEER SOURDOUGH

MAKES 1 loaf
EQUIPMENT 2-pound loaf pan
DF V+

≡

Rye grains are often used in making beer, in place of some of the barley, so the combination of beer and rye is a classic. By using beer to soak the whole grain rye, you really intensify its flavors. It makes a wonderfully flavorsome sandwich with some hard cheese and sauerkraut.

Fermenting our own alcoholic drinks is an aspiration we have for our business, so one day it may be our own beer that goes into this recipe. For many people the thought of having some beer in their bread just brightens the day!

DAY 1

- Scant 1 cup (110 g) light rye flour
- ½ cup (110 g) warm water (90 to 99°F)
- Active Rye Starter (page 42)

Mix the flour and water with the whole quantity of the starter and leave loosely covered at room temperature overnight.

- 7 tablespoons (100 g) beer
- ⅔ cup (100 g) rye grains

Add the beer to the rye grains and let them soak at room temperature overnight.

DAY 2

- Rye and beer mix from Day 1
- 7¾ ounces (220 g) recipe starter from Day 1
- 7 tablespoons (100 g) warm water (90 to 99°F)
- ¼ cup (60 g) beer
- Scant 1 cup (220 g) light rye flour
- 1½ teaspoons (8 g) salt

1. Drain the beer from the rye grains. Discard the beer but keep the rye grains. In a large bowl, combine the recipe starter, warm water, and fresh beer.
2. In another bowl, combine the flour, salt, and rye grains. Always mix the salt into the flour, as salt will kill the active agents, the bacteria and yeast, if it comes into direct contact with them.
3. Add the flour mix to the first bowl and stir well with your hands or a wooden spoon until thoroughly combined. It will be more like a batter than a dough, so kneading won't develop the gluten.
4. Lightly grease a 2-pound loaf pan.
5. Pour the mixture into the pan and smooth over the top.
6. Follow the rest of the Rye Sourdough recipe from Step 6 (page 81) to the end.

RYE, CARAWAY, AND RAISIN SOURDOUGH

MAKES 1 loaf
EQUIPMENT 2-pound loaf pan
DF **V+**

≡

This three-way flavor combination is deeply traditional in northeast Europe. When not prepared properly rye can be quite heavy on the stomach, and caraway has many properties that are believed to aid digestion, which is probably the origin of this combination. Adding raisins brings a sweetness to counterbalance the other slightly bitter flavors.

This is a good breakfast loaf, and is also great for a sweet fix after lunch, toasted, and served with a dollop of honey. Caraway can divide opinion (I am not a great fan myself), so make sure you check with the recipient of the loaf before embarking on this recipe!

DAY 1

- Scant 1 cup (110 g) light rye flour
- ½ cup (110 g) warm water (90 to 99°F)
- Active Rye Starter (page 42)

Mix the flour and water with the whole quantity of the starter and leave loosely covered at room temperature overnight.

- 7 tablespoons (100 g) warm water (90 to 99°F)
- ¾ cup (100 g) raisins

Add the warm water to the raisins and let them soak at room temperature overnight.

DAY 2

- Raisin and water mix from Day 1
- 7¾ ounces (220 g) recipe starter from Day 1
- 7 tablespoons (100 g) warm water (90 to 99°F)
- ¼ cup (60 g) beer
- Scant 1 cup (220 g) light rye flour
- 1½ teaspoons (8 g) salt
- 1 teaspoon (5 g) whole caraway seeds
- Extra caraway seeds and coarse grain salt, for topping

1. Drain the water from the raisins. Discard the water but keep the raisins. In a large bowl, combine the recipe starter, warm water, and beer.

2. In another bowl, combine the flour, salt, raisins, and caraway seeds. Always mix the salt into the flour, as salt will kill the active agents, the bacteria and yeast, if it comes into direct contact with them.

3. Add the flour mix to the first bowl and stir well with your hands or a wooden spoon until thoroughly combined. It will be more like a batter than a dough, so kneading won't develop the gluten.

4. Lightly grease a 2-pound loaf pan.

5. Pour the mixture into the pan and smooth over the top. Top with the extra caraway seeds and a light sprinkling of coarse salt.

6. Follow the rest of the Rye Sourdough recipe from Step 6 (page 81) to the end.

RYE SOURDOUGH WITH RASPBERRIES AND BLACKBERRIES

MAKES 1 loaf **EQUIPMENT** 2-pound loaf pan **DF** **V+**

≡

This one is not an everyday bake, but perfect for when you have that urge to bake something different for family or guests, especially when you've been berry picking. The flavor of rye pairs very well with the natural sweetness of berries. It's a great breakfast toasting bread that avoids the need for jam, but it's also surprisingly delicious as a tartine, under a savory topping, for example salted cod and capers.

DAY 1

- Scant 1 cup (110 g) light rye flour
- ½ cup (110 g) warm water (90 to 99°F)
- Active Rye Starter (page 42)
- ¾ cup (100 g) mixed raspberries and blackberries
- Generous ½ cup (140 g) warm water (90 to 99°F)

Mix the flour and warm water with the whole quantity of the starter and leave loosely covered at room temperature overnight.

Mash the berries slightly and add to the generous ½ cup (140 g) water. Leave overnight in a cool place.

DAY 2

- 7¾ ounces (220 g) recipe starter from Day 1
- Water and berry mix from Day 1
- Scant 1 cup (220 g) light rye flour
- 1½ teaspoons (8 g) salt

1. In a large bowl, combine the recipe starter with the water and berries from Day 1.
2. In another bowl, combine the flour and salt. Always mix the salt into the flour, as salt will kill the active agents, the bacteria and yeast, if it comes into direct contact with them.
3. Add the flour and salt to the first bowl. Stir well with your hands or a wooden spoon until thoroughly combined. It will be more like a batter than a dough, so kneading won't develop the gluten.
4. Lightly grease a 2-pound loaf pan.
5. Pour the mixture into the pan and smooth over the top. Dust with a little more rye flour.
6. Follow the rest of the Rye Sourdough recipe from Step 6 (page 81) to the end.

NUTRITION NOTE

The seeds in berries, even though most are tiny, are a fantastic source of nutrition and are so often overlooked. The seeds' biological function is to act as an energy and nutrient source during germination, hence being packed with goodness.

SPINACH AND SPIRULINA SOURDOUGH

MAKES 1 loaf

EQUIPMENT high-speed blender and oval proofing basket

DF V+

≡

This loaf is an incredibly vibrant green color that makes you feel healthier just by looking at it. Its unusual name raises eyebrows even in our store, where unusual ingredients and pairings are commonplace. It's a really good example of how far you can push bread, flavors, and nutrition. It's not hard to make, yet it's this sort of bread making that makes us Modern Baker. It's the perfect accompaniment to soup or salad, makes an exotic-looking chunky green sandwich, or you can simply serve it as a conversation piece all on its own.

DAY 1

- 6 tablespoons (50 g) white bread flour
- 3½ tablespoons (50 g) warm water (90 to 99°F)
- Active Wheat Starter (page 41)

Add the flour and warm water to the whole quantity of the starter and leave loosely covered overnight at room temperature.

DAY 2

- 3½ ounces (100 g) fresh spinach leaves
- Scant 1 cup (225 g) warm water (90 to 99°F)
- 3½ ounces (100 g) recipe starter from Day 1
- 3½ cups (500 g) white bread flour
- 2 teaspoons (10 g) spirulina powder
- ¼ teaspoon (1 g) grated nutmeg
- 1½ teaspoons (8 g) salt

1 In a high-speed blender, blitz the spinach with the warm water until completely blended.

2 In a large bowl, combine the recipe starter with the spinach water and mix gently.

3 In another bowl, combine the flour with the spirulina powder, nutmeg, and salt.

4 Add the flour and spirulina mix to the first bowl and mix using one hand until a dough forms. This takes only a couple of minutes. It's a good idea to use only one hand, leaving the other one clean for using utensils, etc. Use a plastic dough scraper around the bowl to make sure all the flour is mixed in. Cover the bowl with a shower cap or damp dish towel and let it rest.

5 After 5 to 10 minutes, give the dough a fold in the bowl. Use slightly wet hands to prevent the dough sticking to them. Pull a section of the dough out to the side and fold it into the middle of the ball. Repeat this going around the ball of dough until you get back to the beginning (four or five folds). Use the scraper to turn the dough upside down, cover the bowl, and leave for another 5 to 10 minutes. Repeat this three times.

After the final fold, cover the bowl again and let rest for 1 hour.

6 Turn the dough out of the bowl onto a lightly floured counter. Stretch out one side of the dough and fold it into the middle. Repeat this with each of the four "sides" of the dough. Put the dough back in the bowl upside down and let rest for another hour.

7 Follow the rest of the Basic Sourdough recipe from Step 6 (page 46) to the end, but bake for an additional 10 minutes.

NUTRITION NOTE

Spinach's qualities are well known. It's rich in proteins and fiber and is a source of vitamins A and C and folic acid. Spirulina, derived from algae and technically a bacteria rather than a plant, is much more mysterious, and possibly even more valuable as it contains some of nature's less commonly found nutrients.

TARTINES

SERVES 2

EQUIPMENT 1 or 2 baking sheets

As a bakery, we couldn't put together this recipe book without including a few tartines and pizzas, both of which are as embedded in bread culture as butter. A good sourdough transforms both of these into another league, it brings the toppings to life and soaks up the flavors. Our eyes were opened to the never-ending variety of possible toppings with the arrival of Ashley, our "beyond baking" chef, who has developed some fabulous flavor combos to go with the sourdoughs.

AVOCADO, FETA, BLACK OLIVE, RED ONION, AND OREGANO TARTINE

- 2 slices sourdough bread
- 1 ripe medium avocado
- ¼ red onion, minced
- Juice of ½ lemon
- Salt and freshly ground black pepper
- 1¾ ounces (50 g) feta, crumbled
- 6 pitted black olives, sliced
- 1 sprig fresh oregano leaves

1 Chargrill or toast the bread. Peel and pit the avocado into a bowl.

2 Add the onion, lemon juice, and a pinch (0.25 g) of salt and pepper. Gently mash with a fork, check the seasoning, then spread onto the toast.

3 Sprinkle the feta, olives, and oregano over the top.

BRUSSELS SPROUTS, COCONUT BACON, FETA, AND HAZELNUTS TARTINE

FOR THE COCONUT BACON (THIS WILL MAKE EXTRA)

- 2 tablespoons (25 g) tamari
- 1 tablespoon (15 g) maple syrup
- ½ teaspoon (2.5 g) smoked paprika
- 5 cups (250 g) large-flaked coconut

1 Preheat the oven to 375°F and line 1 or 2 baking sheets with parchment paper.

2 In a bowl, combine all the coconut bacon ingredients, except for the coconut. Add the coconut and massage it in the liquid until all covered.

3 Spread onto the baking sheets and put in the oven. It should take 25 minutes, but move the coconut around every 5 minutes or so.

4 Once golden, remove and let cool. It will crisp up. Keep in a sealed container.

FOR THE TARTINE

- 2 slices sourdough bread
- 1 tablespoon (15 g) coconut oil
- 7 ounces (200 g) Brussels sprouts, shredded
- 1¾ ounces (50 g) feta, crumbled
- Scant ½ cup (50 g) hazelnuts, crushed
- Coconut bacon (see above)

5 Chargrill or toast the sourdough.

6 Heat the oil in a skillet. Add the sprouts and fry until golden and crispy. Remove from the heat and toss in the feta, nuts, and coconut bacon.

GLUTEN-FREE SEEDED SOURDOUGH

≡

This was the first gluten-free loaf we created for the bakery. It is an amalgamation of many different recipes we tried and rejected along the way. Making this loaf taught us so much about gluten-free baking, especially about the different gluten-free flours there are available (page 25).

We soon learned that rather than relying on ready-made blends, we preferred to make our own blends as it gave us more control over the final texture and flavor of both our gluten-free breads and our cakes. Over time we have developed more gluten-free loaves, but this is still our most popular. If you are struggling to find teff flour you can replace it with quinoa flour, or use more buckwheat flour.

Many of our gluten-free customers tell us that this is the closest they've come to "normal" bread, and actually many people who don't need to be gluten-free buy it too. The seeds add a significant nutritional boost as well as providing texture.

DAY 1

- ¾ cup (100 g) brown rice flour
- 7 tablespoons (100 g) warm water (90 to 99°F)
- Active Gluten-Free Brown Rice Starter (page 42)

Add the flour and warm water to the whole quantity of the starter and leave loosely covered overnight at room temperature.

DAY 2

- 7 ounces (200 g) recipe starter from Day 1
- 1¼ cups (300 g) warm water (90 to 99°F)
- 1¼ cups (150 g) buckwheat flour
- ⅔ cup (100 g) potato or tapioca flour
- Scant ½ cup (50 g) teff flour
- 1½ teaspoons (8 g) salt
- 1 cup (140 g) mixed seeds (we like to use sunflower, pumpkin, sesame, and flaxseed)

MAKES 1 loaf **EQUIPMENT** 2-pound loaf pan **GF DF V+**

1. In a large bowl, mix together the recipe starter and the warm water.
2. In another bowl, mix together the flours, salt, and seeds.
3. Add the flour mix to the first bowl and mix well, with either your hand or a wooden spoon. You are not trying to develop any gluten, so there is no need to mix for too long. It should resemble a thick batter.
4. Cover the bowl with a damp dish towel or shower cap and let rest for 1 hour at room temperature.
5. Lightly grease a 2-pound loaf pan.
6. Pour the batter into the pan and smooth over the top with a wet dough scraper. At this stage you have two options, you can leave it in the refrigerator (covered with a damp dish towel) to bake the next day, or you can leave it at room temperature until it has reached the top of the pan (about 2 to 4 hours) and bake it the same day. By leaving it overnight you improve the temperature and health benefits of the sourdough, so this is what we always do and what we recommend, but if you need the bread sooner, baking it the same day will still produce a delicious loaf.
7. Preheat the oven to 500°F. Place a roasting pan in the bottom of the oven to heat up. Fill a cup with water and place to one side ready to use.

   At this stage, if you notice that the loaf has started to form a dry crust over the top just brush it lightly with water and let it absorb it while the oven warms up.

   Unlike loaves with gluten, gluten-free bread does not need slashing before baking.
8. Place the pan in the oven and pour the glass of water into the roasting pan. This will help give a lovely crust and create a lighter loaf.
9. Turn the temperature down to 475°F and bake for 30 to 40 minutes. To check that the loaf is baked through, turn it out of the pan and tap the bottom—it should sound hollow. If not, return it to the oven for another 5 to 10 minutes.
10. Once baked, turn the loaf out onto a wire rack straightaway. Let cool for at least 1 hour before eating, as the bread will still be cooking and the starch settling.

GLUTEN-FREE CHICKPEA SOURDOUGH

MAKES 1 loaf
EQUIPMENT 2-pound loaf pan
GF DF V+

The first thing that will strike you about this loaf is its fantastic golden orange color. It really stands out among all the other, traditional-looking loaves. Its distinctive chickpea flavor may make you question what to eat it with, but it's actually surprisingly versatile. Our favorite ways to have it are with avocado, fresh tomato, and a sprinkling of red pepper flakes, or some tahini (sesame seed paste) and a drizzle of raw honey.

We don't use chickpea flour (often sold as gram flour) on its own as that would produce a very heavy loaf with an overwhelming flavor. Instead we mix it with buckwheat and tapioca flour, and base it on our brown rice flour starter.

NUTRITION NOTE

We created this loaf because we were looking for a GF alternative that was higher in protein. It comes with the added benefit of being low glycemic index as well. Technically, this is one of our most interesting loaves.

DAY 1

- ¾ cup (100 g) brown rice flour
- 7 tablespoons (100 g) warm water (90 to 99°F)
- Active Gluten-Free Brown Rice Starter (page 42)

Add the flour and the water to the whole quantity of the starter and leave at room temperature overnight.

DAY 2

- 7 ounces (200 g) recipe starter from Day 1
- 1¼ cups (300 g) warm water (90 to 99°F)
- 1¼ cups (150 g) chickpea/gram flour
- Generous ¾ cup (100 g) buckwheat flour
- 1½ cups (170 g) tapioca flour
- 1½ teaspoons (8 g) Himalayan pink salt, finely ground

1. In a large bowl, mix the recipe starter with the water.
2. In another bowl, combine the flours with the salt and mix well. It is important to mix the flours together well, as any lumps will become unpleasant patches in the baked loaf.
3. Add the flour mix to the first bowl and stir well, with either your hands or a wooden spoon. You are not trying to develop any gluten, so there is no need to mix for too long.
4. Cover the bowl with a damp dish towel or shower cap and let rest for 1 hour at room temperature.
5. Lightly grease a 2-pound loaf pan.
6. Follow the rest of the Gluten-Free Seeded Sourdough recipe from Step 6 (page 92) to the end. The loaf can be eaten as soon as it is cool.

GLUTEN-FREE NUTTY SOURDOUGH

MAKES 1 loaf
EQUIPMENT 2-pound loaf pan
GF DF V+

≡

This is a brand-new loaf, the result of combining two of our most popular ingredients—nuts and seeds—into a gluten-free loaf. We have to say, it's been an instant hit. A regular gluten-free customer, who is not easily pleased, has given it 10 out of 10.

This is a perfect example of what excites us about healthy baking, using modern knowledge and baking capabilities with the ancient arts of fermentation and bread making. We are barely into our journey, yet not a day passes when another combination doesn't come to mind, always based on our core principles of provenance, nutrition, and taste.

This loaf is incredibly nutty, which helps to add to the protein and healthy fats. It has a creamy, mellow undertone from the almond and tapioca combination, and we find it goes particularly well with some strong cheese and thinly sliced apple, or roasted butternut squash and kale.

DAY 1

- ¾ cup (100 g) brown rice flour
- 7 tablespoons (100 g) warm water (90 to 99°F)
- Active Gluten-Free Brown Rice Starter (page 42)

Add the flour and the water to the whole quantity of the starter and leave at room temperature overnight.

DAY 2

- 7 ounces (200 g) recipe starter from Day 1
- 1¼ cups (300 g) warm water (90 to 99°F)
- Generous ¾ cup (100 g) buckwheat flour
- ½ cup (65 g) tapioca flour
- ⅔ cup (65 g) hazelnut meal
- ½ cup (50 g) almond meal
- ¾ cup (100 g) walnuts, chopped
- 1½ teaspoons (8 g) salt

1. In a large bowl, mix together the recipe starter and water.
2. In another bowl, mix together the flours, nuts, and salt.
3. Add the flour mix to the first bowl and stir well, either with your hands or a wooden spoon. You are not trying to develop any gluten, so there is no need to mix for too long.
4. Cover the bowl with a damp dish towel or shower cap and let rest for 1 hour at room temperature.
5. Lightly grease a 2-pound loaf pan.
6. Follow the rest of the Gluten-Free Seeded Sourdough recipe from Step 6 (page 92) to the end. This loaf can be eaten as soon as it is cool enough.

GLUTEN-FREE SOURDOUGH FLATBREADS

≡

These gluten-free sourdough flatbreads are perfect for eating with dips. The chickpea flour in them particularly complements hummus. While our gluten-free sourdough breads are made with almost a batter mix, these have more of a dough. You can add spices and herbs if desired, we like to use cumin seeds or rosemary.

This is a really good option for when you're catering for lots of people and you don't want to have to ask everyone in advance if they are gluten-free.

DAY 1

- ⅓ cup (50 g) brown rice flour
- 3½ tablespoons (50 g) warm water (90 to 99°F)
- Active Gluten-Free Brown Rice Starter (page 42)

Add the flour and the water to the whole quantity of the starter and leave at room temperature overnight.

DAY 2

- 3½ ounces (100 g) recipe starter from Day 1
- Scant 1 cup (220 g) warm water (90 to 99°F)
- 7 tablespoons (100 g) almond milk (or other milk of your choice)
- 3½ tablespoons (50 g) extra virgin olive oil
- Scant 1½ cups (180 g) chickpea flour
- 1 cup (120 g) tapioca flour
- 1¼ cups (150 g) buckwheat flour
- 1½ teaspoons (8 g) salt
- Olive or sunflower oil, for brushing

1. In a large bowl, mix together the recipe starter with the water, milk, and oil.
2. In another bowl, combine the three flours and the salt.
3. Add the flours to the first bowl and mix well with your hands until it comes together in a dough. Cover the bowl with a damp dish towel or shower cap and let it rest in the refrigerator overnight.
4. The next day, divide the dough into eight equal pieces. Roll the dough pieces into balls.
5. On a lightly floured counter, roll the balls out flat, to about 8-inch circles.
6. Heat a large skillet over medium heat and very lightly brush it with oil.
7. Carefully transfer one flatbread to the pan. Cook until it starts to puff, about 1 minute, then flip it over and cook for another minute, until golden.
8. Transfer it to a plate and cover with parchment paper. Repeat for the rest of the flatbreads. You can either eat them straightaway or let them rest, but they are best eaten on the same day.

MAKES 8 flatbreads **EQUIPMENT** skillet **GF** **DF** **V+**

GLUTEN-FREE LOW-GI SUPER SOURDOUGH

MAKES 1 loaf
EQUIPMENT 2-pound loaf pan
GF DF V+

≡

Many gluten-free flours are quite high on the glycemic index (GI), potato being a good example. So when our customer Natalia, who is a nutritionist, asked if it was possible for us make a gluten-free loaf with a low GI, we set to work. The challenge was avoiding bitter flavors, but eventually the combination of buckwheat, millet, tapioca, and quinoa flours along with oats and whole quinoa proved to be the winning formula. The tapioca was the key to getting the right texture.

Long fermenting substantially reduces GI levels anyway, so this loaf more than answers Natalia's brief (although we are yet to have it officially tested). GI levels are coming under more and more scrutiny, especially for people faced with diabetes. Australia is leading the way on GI food product labeling and it will reach other countries over time. It's an area we are especially interested in, as is our local university's Functional Food department.

DAY 1

- 7 tablespoons (100 g) warm water (90 to 99°F)
- ¾ cup (100 g) brown rice flour
- Active Gluten-Free Brown Rice Starter (page 42)

Add the water and flour to the whole quantity of the starter and leave loosely covered overnight at room temperature.

DAY 2

- 7 ounces (200 g) recipe starter from Day 1
- 1¾ cups (400 g) warm water (90 to 99°F)
- Generous ¾ cup (100 g) buckwheat flour
- ½ cup (65 g) tapioca flour
- ½ cup (65 g) quinoa flour
- Scant ½ cup (50 g) millet flour
- ½ cup (50 g) oats
- ½ cup (50 g) quinoa flakes
- 1½ teaspoons (8 g) salt

1. In a large bowl, mix together the recipe starter and water.
2. In another bowl, mix together the flours, oats, quinoa flakes, and salt.
3. Add the flour mix to the first bowl and stir well, either with your hands or a wooden spoon. You are not trying to develop any gluten, so there is no need to mix for too long.
4. Cover the bowl with a damp dish towel or shower cap and let rest for 1 hour at room temperature.
5. Lightly grease a 2-pound loaf pan.
6. Follow the rest of the Gluten-Free Seeded Sourdough recipe from Step 6 (page 92) to the end. This loaf can be eaten as soon as it is cool.

GLUTEN-FREE CHOCOLATE, RAISIN, AND HAZELNUT SOURDOUGH

MAKES 1 loaf
EQUIPMENT 2-pound loaf pan
GF DF V+

The spelt version of this loaf is one of our most popular specials, so much so that our customers asked if we could create a gluten-free version as well. If it stays around for long enough, we recommend slicing and freezing it so you can pull a slice out whenever you fancy a quick chocolate fix.

Toast a slice of this loaf and enjoy it with some butter or hazelnut butter. This is neither cake nor bread, it's your answer to that toasted teacake moment, and although they bring indulgence to this recipe, cacao powder and hazelnuts are also packed with goodness.

For chocolate lovers, and bakers, it's really fundamental to know that cacao powder is not cocoa powder. Cacao is cold-pressed, raw cocoa beans, while cocoa powder is made from roasted beans. Unfortunately, roasting removes some of the goodness.

DAY 1

- 7 tablespoons (100 g) warm water (90 to 99°F)
- ¾ cup (100 g) brown rice flour
- Active Gluten-Free Brown Rice Starter (page 42)

Add the water and flour to the whole quantity of the starter and leave loosely covered overnight at room temperature.

NUTRITION NOTE

Cacao is antioxidant-rich and is known as a "feel-good" food because research has shown that it can help to reduce anxiety and improve mood. It's also packed with minerals, and lowers the body's insulin resistance.

DAY 2

- 7 ounces (200 g) recipe starter from Day 1
- 1¼ cups (300 g) warm water (90 to 99°F)
- Scant 1 cup (100 g) tapioca flour
- 1¼ cups (150 g) buckwheat flour
- ½ cup (50 g) raw cacao powder
- ⅔ cup (100 g) coconut sugar–sweetened chocolate chips, but if you cannot find these use your favorite healthy semisweet chocolate
- ¾ cup (100 g) whole hazelnuts
- ¾ cup (100 g) raisins
- 1½ teaspoons (8 g) salt

1. In a large bowl, mix together the recipe starter and water.
2. In another bowl, mix together the flours, cacao, chocolate chips, hazelnuts, raisins, and salt.
3. Add the flour mix to the first bowl and stir well, either with your hands or a wooden spoon. You are not trying to develop any gluten, so there is no need to mix for too long.
4. Cover the bowl with a damp dish towel or shower cap and let rest for 1 hour at room temperature.
5. Lightly grease a 2-pound loaf pan.
6. Follow the rest of the Gluten-Free Seeded Sourdough recipe from Step 6 (page 92) to the end, baking for 40 minutes. This loaf can be eaten as soon as it is cool enough.

GLUTEN-FREE SUNDRIED TOMATO AND BASIL SOURDOUGH

≡

This is an adaptation of our chickpea sourdough. We use sundried tomatoes that you need to rehydrate, as soaking them in water and then using that water in the bread really intensifies the flavor. This combination of flavors makes a brilliant loaf to take on a picnic; all you need is a drizzle of olive oil for a delicious savory treat.

DAY 1

- 7 tablespoons (100 g) warm water (90 to 99°F)
- ¾ cup (100 g) brown rice flour
- Active Gluten-Free Brown Rice Starter (page 42)

Add the water and flour to the whole quantity of the starter and leave loosely covered overnight at room temperature.

- 1⅔ cups (100 g) sundried tomatoes, chopped into small pieces
- 1¾ cups (400 g) warm water (90 to 99°F)

Soak the sundried tomatoes in the water and leave at room temperature overnight.

DAY 2

- 7 ounces (200 g) recipe starter from Day 1
- Sundried tomato and water mix from Day 1
- 1¼ cups (150 g) chickpea/gram flour
- Generous ¾ cup (100 g) buckwheat flour
- 1½ cups (170 g) tapioca flour
- 1½ teaspoons (8 g) Himalayan pink salt, finely ground
- Handful of fresh basil, finely chopped

1. In a large bowl, mix together the recipe starter with the sundried tomato and water mix from Day 1.
2. In another bowl, combine the flours with the salt and basil and mix well. It is important to mix the flours together well, as any lumps will become unpleasant patches in the baked loaf.
3. Add the flour mix to the first bowl and stir well, with either your hands or a wooden spoon. You are not trying to develop any gluten, so there is no need to mix for too long.
4. Cover the bowl with a damp dish towel or shower cap and let rest for 1 hour at room temperature.
5. Lightly grease a 2-pound loaf pan.
6. Follow the rest of the Gluten-Free Seeded Sourdough recipe from Step 6 (page 92) to the end, baking for 45 minutes. This loaf can be eaten as soon as it is cool enough.

NUTRITION NOTE

Breads with higher protein levels like this one do command quite a following, especially for people who try to eat protein at every single meal, like me!

MAKES 1 loaf **EQUIPMENT** 2-pound loaf pan **GF DF V+**

SOURDOUGH CINNAMON AND PECAN BUNS

MAKES 8 rolls **EQUIPMENT** 10½ × 8-inch brownie tray

≡

These have been on the Modern Baker counter since our first day, and have been one of our biggest hits. They are quite decadent and delicious; the coconut sugar gives a real caramel hit, which works perfectly with the cinnamon and the butteriness of the butter and pecans. You can't beat these for a lazy breakfast in bed. We make double batches on weekends, and they're often gone by 10. They also seem to be a staple for that Friday office treat.

Cinnamon tricks the palate into thinking it's something sweet, so not only does it have nutritional benefits, it's a really useful ingredient and one we use a lot. We call pecans posh walnuts because they are more expensive, and the reason we use them in these buns is because they hold their crunch so well.

DAY 1

- 8½ tablespoons (75 g) white bread flour
- 5 tablespoons (75 g) warm water (90 to 99°F)
- Active Wheat Starter (page 41)

Add the flour and water to the whole quantity of the starter and leave loosely covered overnight at room temperature.

DAY 2

- 5½ ounces (150 g) recipe starter from Day 1
- Generous 1¼ cups (325 g) whole milk
- 3½ cups (500 g) white bread flour
- 5 teaspoons (25 g) coconut sugar
- Scant 1 teaspoon (5 g) salt
- 2 tablespoons (25 g) unsalted butter

FOR THE FILLING

- ¼ cup (50 g) coconut sugar
- 1 tablespoon (15 g) ground cinnamon
- 2 tablespoons (25 g) unsalted butter
- Scant 1 cup (100 g) pecans, coarsely chopped
- Maple syrup, for glazing the top

1. In a large bowl, combine the recipe starter with the milk and mix gently.

2. In another bowl, combine the flour, sugar, and salt.

3. Add the flour mix to the first bowl and combine until it comes together in a dough. Cover the bowl with a damp dish towel or shower cap and let rest.

→

4 After 5 to 10 minutes, give the dough a fold in the bowl. Use slightly wet hands to prevent the dough sticking to them. Pull a section of the dough out to the side and fold it into the middle of the ball. Repeat this going around the ball of dough until you get back to the beginning (four or five folds). Use the scraper to turn the dough upside down, cover the bowl, and leave for another 5 to 10 minutes. Repeat this another two times. For the third and final fold, add the butter, folding well and making sure the butter is fully combined with the dough. If you add the butter before this point, it can stop the gluten developing. After the final fold, cover the bowl again and let it rest for 1 hour at room temperature.

5 After an hour, give the dough another fold and leave for another hour, this time in the refrigerator.

6 In a bowl, combine the sugar and cinnamon for the filling, and in a pan melt the butter. Line a brownie tray with parchment paper.

7 Turn the dough out onto a lightly floured counter and roll it out to about 12½ × 9½ inches. Brush two-thirds of the melted butter over the dough, leaving a gap of ¾ inch at the bottom to help the dough to seal when you roll it up. Sprinkle the cinnamon sugar over the butter. Spread the pecans over the top.

8 Roll up the dough toward you. As you roll, push the dough back, then pull it forward to get the roll as tight as possible. You will end up with a long log.

9 Brush the top of the log with the remaining melted butter. This will make the buns easier to divide when they are baked.

10 Cut the log into eight equal pieces, each about 1½ inches wide. Place the buns swirl side up in the brownie tray and press down well on each one.

11 At this point put them in the refrigerator, covered with a damp dish towel or shower cap, and leave overnight.

12 In the morning, preheat the oven to 500°F. When the oven is up to temperature, take the buns out of the refrigerator and put them straight in the oven.

13 Turn the temperature down to 450°F and bake for 20 to 25 minutes until the tops are an even golden color.

14 As soon as the buns come out the oven, brush them with a thin layer of maple syrup. Let them cool on the tray for at least 30 minutes before eating.

SAVORY PESTO AND WALNUT SOURDOUGH BUNS

MAKES 8 rolls

EQUIPMENT 10½ × 8-inch brownie tray

DF

≡

Here's another great change from bread, and a delicious savory treat. Pesto and walnuts are often paired and for good reason, they produce wonderful umami flavors that are further enhanced by the sourdough tang. We make our own pesto using seaweed flakes and walnuts, both high in nutritional value as well as giving a flavor boost. You could also add some crumbled feta to the filling. These are perfect for picnics or as a side with soup.

DAY 1

- 8½ tablespoons (75 g) white bread flour
- 5 tablespoons (75 g) warm water (90 to 99°F)
- Active Wheat Starter (page 41)

Add the flour and water to the whole quantity of the starter and leave loosely covered overnight at room temperature.

DAY 2

- 5½ ounces (150 g) recipe starter from Day 1
- 1⅓ cups (320 g) warm water (90 to 99°F)
- 3½ cups (500 g) sprouted whole wheat flour
- 1 teaspoon (6 g) salt
- 2 tablespoons (25 g) olive oil

FOR THE FILLING

- 5 tablespoons Pesto (page 60)
- ¾ cup (100 g) walnuts
- 2 tablespoons (25 g) extra virgin olive oil, for glazing the top

1. In a large bowl, combine the recipe starter with the water and mix gently.

2. In another bowl, combine the flour and salt.

3. Add the flour mix to the first bowl and combine well with your hands until it comes together in a dough. Cover the bowl with a damp dish towel or shower cap and let it rest.

4. After 5 to 10 minutes, give the dough a fold in the bowl. Use slightly wet hands to prevent the dough sticking to them. Pull a section of the dough out to the side and fold it into the middle of the ball. Repeat this going

→

around the ball of dough until you get back to the beginning (four or five folds). Use the scraper to turn the dough upside down, cover the bowl, and leave for another 5 to 10 minutes. Repeat this another two times.

Fold once again, this time adding the olive oil, folding well and making sure the oil is fully combined with the dough. If you add the oil before this point, it can stop the gluten developing.

After the final fold, cover the bowl again and let it rest for 1 hour at room temperature.

5 After an hour give the dough another fold and leave for another hour in the refrigerator.

6 Line a brownie tray with parchment paper.

7 Turn the dough out onto a lightly floured counter and roll it out to about 12½ × 9½ inches. Spread the pesto over the top of the dough leaving a ¾-inch gap at the bottom. Spread the walnuts over the top of the pesto.

8 Roll up the dough toward you. As you roll, push the dough back, then pull it forward to get the roll as tight as possible. You will end up with a long log.

9 Brush the top of the log with the olive oil. This will make the buns easier to divide when they are baked.

10 Cut the log into eight equal pieces, each about 1½ inches wide. Place the buns swirl side up in the brownie tray and press down well on each one.

11 Follow the rest of the Sourdough Cinnamon and Pecan Buns recipe from Step 11 (page 104) to the end, brushing with a thin layer of olive oil when they come out of the oven.

COCONUT AND LEMON CURD SOURDOUGH BUNS

≡

The name and ingredient list makes these buns sound more like cakes, but they are definitely not. We created them for customers who love the idea of a sourdough bun but don't like the flavor of cinnamon; it's definitely a spice not to everyone's liking. We always make our own lemon curd; it's very easy and you can always make an extra batch for the refrigerator.

The lemon zest carries these buns—we thought it might clash with the piquancy of the sourdough, but in fact they work together surprisingly well. These are a delicious, fresh, zingy breakfast treat.

DAY 1

- 8½ tablespoons (75 g) white bread flour
- 5 tablespoons (75 g) warm water (90 to 99°F)
- Active Wheat Starter (page 41)

Add the flour and water to the whole quantity of the starter and leave loosely covered overnight at room temperature.

LEMON CURD

- 3 extra-large eggs
- ¼ cup (80 g) honey
- Zest of 2 lemons, grated
- ¼ cup (55 g) coconut oil
- Juice of 2 lemons

Put all the ingredients in a small pan and stir over low heat until thick. This can take 10 to 15 minutes. Transfer the hot mixture to an airtight container or a sterilized jar.

DAY 2

- 5½ ounces (150 g) recipe starter from Day 1
- Generous 1¼ cups (325 g) warm coconut milk
- 3¼ cups (450 g) white bread flour
- ⅓ cup (50 g) whole wheat flour
- Scant 1 teaspoon (5 g) salt
- Zest of 1 lemon, grated
- 4 teaspoons (20 g) coconut oil, softened
- 2 tablespoons (25 g) honey

FOR THE FILLING

- 5 tablespoons (75 g) Lemon Curd (see above)
- Scant ½ cup (50 g) goji berries
- Scant ½ cup (50 g) raisins
- Coconut oil, melted, for glazing the top
- 1 tablespoon (15 g) honey, for glazing the top

MAKES 8 rolls **EQUIPMENT** 10½ × 8-inch brownie tray **DF**

1 In a large bowl, combine the recipe starter with the milk and mix gently.

2 In another bowl, combine the flours, salt, and lemon zest.

3 Add the flours to the first bowl and combine well with your hands until it comes together in a dough. Cover the bowl with a damp dish towel or shower cap and let it rest.

4 After 5 to 10 minutes, give the dough a fold in the bowl. Use slightly wet hands to prevent the dough sticking to them. Pull a section of the dough out to the side and fold it into the middle of the ball. Repeat this going around the ball of dough until you get back to the beginning (four or five folds). Use the scraper to turn the dough upside down, cover the bowl, and leave for another 5 to 10 minutes. Repeat this another two times. Fold one more time, this time adding the oil and honey, fold well, and make sure the oil and honey are fully combined with the dough. If you add the oil before this point it can stop the gluten developing. After the final fold cover the bowl again and let rest for 1 hour at room temperature.

5 After an hour, give the dough another fold and leave for another hour in the refrigerator.

6 Line a brownie tray with parchment paper.

7 Turn the dough out onto a lightly floured counter and roll it out to about 12½ × 9½ inches. Spread the lemon curd over the dough, leaving a ¾-inch gap at the bottom. Sprinkle the goji berries and raisins over the top.

8 Roll up the dough toward you. As you roll, push the dough back, then pull it forward to get the roll as tight as possible. You will end up with a long log.

9 Brush the top of the log with the melted oil. This will make the buns easier to divide when they are baked.

10 Cut the log into eight equal pieces, each about 1½ inches wide. Place the buns swirl side up in the brownie tray and press down well on each one.

11 Follow the rest of the Sourdough Cinnamon and Pecan Buns recipe from Step 11 (page 104) to the end, brushing with a thin layer of honey when they come out of the oven.

SOURDOUGH PITA BREAD

≡

Pita breads are so much easier to make than most people realize. And the sourdough flavor here makes such a difference. They are delicious pillows of chewiness ready to be stuffed with anything you fancy, and can be frozen if you don't eat them all straightaway.

We love them, filled with garden salad, alfalfa sprouts, broiled halloumi, and an avocado and olive oil dressing with a hint of lemon juice.

DAY 1

- 2¾ tablespoons (25 g) white bread flour
- 2 tablespoons (25 g) warm water (90 to 99°F)
- Active Wheat Starter (page 41)

Mix the flour and water with the whole quantity of the starter and leave loosely covered at room temperature overnight.

DAY 2

- 1¾ ounces (50 g) recipe starter from Day 1
- ½ cup (125 g) warm water (90 to 99°F)
- About 1¾ cups (250 g) white bread flour
- Scant 1 teaspoon (5 g) salt
- 4 teaspoons (20 g) olive oil (not extra virgin as the flavor is too strong)

MAKES 9 small pita breads **EQUIPMENT** baking sheet **DF V+**

1. In a large bowl, combine the recipe starter with the warm water and mix gently.

2. In another bowl, mix together the flour and salt.

3. Add the flour mix to the first bowl and combine well with your hands until it comes together into a dough. Cover the bowl with a damp dish towel or shower cap and let rest.

4. After 5 to 10 minutes, give the dough a fold in the bowl. Use slightly wet hands to prevent the dough sticking to them. Pull a section of the dough out to the side and fold it into the middle of the ball. Repeat this going around the ball of dough until you get back to the beginning (four or five folds). Use the scraper to turn the dough upside down, cover the bowl, and leave for another 5 to 10 minutes. Repeat this another three times. Fold one more time, this time adding the olive oil, fold well, and make sure the oil is fully combined with the dough. If you add the oil before this point it can stop the gluten developing. After the final fold, cover the bowl again and let rest for 1 hour at room temperature.

5. Turn the dough out of the bowl onto a lightly floured counter. Stretch out one side of the dough and fold it into the middle. Repeat this with each of the four "sides" of the dough. Put the dough back in the bowl upside down and let rest for another hour.

6. **Shaping pitas:** Divide the dough into nine pieces (about 1¾ ounces each) and roll them into balls. Rest them on a floured sheet with space between each one. At this stage you can either leave them in the refrigerator overnight covered in a damp dish towel, or rest them at room temperature for an hour.

7. When you are ready to bake, preheat the oven to 500°F and place a baking sheet on the middle shelf to heat up.

8. Place the balls on a lightly floured counter and roll them out into long oval shapes.

9. When the oven is up to temperature, bake the pitas in batches of three by carefully laying them on the heated baking sheet. Bake for 2 to 3 minutes until they start to pop, then flip them over and bake for another 2 minutes. Repeat with all the pitas.

10. Let the pitas cool on a wire rack. You can eat them warm or keep them in a breathable container until required. Alternatively, you can freeze them once cold.

SOURDOUGH PIZZA

≡

Pizza is now a staple of the modern diet, seemingly all over the world. These delicious sourdough pizza bases are a great starting place for all new healthy bakers, especially young ones. And making a pizza with a healthy base from stone-ground flour and natural fermentation is all you need to spur you into taking the same care over the toppings.

This pizza base is Leo's children's absolute favorite and a regular request from our baking team when they're around. We keep a stash of ready-to-go pizza dough balls in the freezer. Transfer them to the refrigerator the night before you need them.

We use the same dough as for our pita breads for this recipe, but you could use the Sprouted Whole Wheat dough (page 66) instead, just add a little olive oil on the final fold of the mixing stage. We have suggested our favorite pizza toppings.

PIZZA BASE

- Gluten-free sourdough flatbreads, but made with 2 tablespoons (30 g) olive oil (not extra virgin as the flavor is too strong) (page 96)

VARIATION

GLUTEN-FREE SOURDOUGH PIZZA BASE

There are an increasing number of gluten-free pizza base recipes out there, but we struggled to find one that did not contain potato flour (high glycemic index), and there were none for sourdough. Our Gluten-Free Sourdough Pita Bread dough (page 110) is the result of plenty of trial and error and is a brilliant pizza base. The recipe makes enough dough for eight medium pizzas. We think it's another example of a gluten-free bake that tastes easily as good as its gluten counterpart.

SHAPING PIZZA BASES

Divide the dough into four equal pieces and roll them into balls. Rest them on a floured sheet with space between each one. At this stage you can either leave them in the refrigerator overnight covered in a damp dish towel or rest them at room temperature for an hour.

MAKES 4 medium pizza bases and tomato sauce, either refrigerate for 3 days or freeze

TOMATO SAUCE

This is a basic tomato sauce to sit on the pizza base and under any other topping of your choice. One of our recipes overleaf does not require a tomato sauce base.

- 2¼ pounds (1 kg) whole tomatoes, cored
- 1 onion, finely diced
- 2 tablespoons (25 g) grapeseed oil
- 2 garlic cloves, finely sliced
- 1 tablespoon (15 g) tomato paste
- Salt and freshly ground black pepper
- 1 tablespoon (15 g) fresh basil, chopped
- 1 tablespoon (15 g) fresh oregano, chopped

1. Bring a large pot of water to a boil. Make a small X in the bottom of each tomato and plunge into the boiling water until the skins are slightly loosened, about 30 seconds. Transfer to a bowl of ice water for 1 minute. Peel with a paring knife, starting at the X, then chop, keeping any juice.

2. In a pan over low heat, gently cook the onion in the oil until it starts to go translucent. Add the garlic and after 1 minute the tomatoes and juice and tomato paste. Season with salt and pepper and let simmer for 1 hour, or until reduced and thickened. Add the herbs and check the seasoning again.

CHOICE OF TOPPINGS (SEE OVERLEAF)

MAKES 2 medium pizzas
EQUIPMENT 2 flat baking sheets or pizza stones

ROAST BUTTERNUT SQUASH, GOAT CHEESE, WALNUTS, ARUGULA, AND POMEGRANATE PIZZA

- 10½ ounces (300 g) butternut squash, peeled and cubed
- Grapeseed oil and salt, for roasting
- 4½ ounces (125 g) crumbly goat cheese
- ½ cup (60 g) chopped walnuts
- 2 cups (50 g) arugula
- Scant ½ cup (60 g) pomegranate seeds
- Extra virgin olive oil, for drizzling

1. Preheat the oven to 425°F.
2. Place the squash on a baking sheet and drizzle with oil and salt. Toss to coat and roast for 20 minutes, tossing halfway through.
3. Once roasted, raise the oven temperature to its maximum heat and place two flat baking sheets or pizza stones on the middle shelf to heat up.
4. Place two of the dough balls on a sheet of parchment paper. This makes transferring them to the oven easier. Roll them out to your desired size and spread with the squash. Crumble over the goat cheese and walnuts.
5. When the oven is up to temperature, bake the pizzas one at a time on the hot baking sheet or stone. Bake for 10 to 12 minutes until the base is crispy and the toppings are golden, keeping an eye that the crust does not burn.
6. Remove from the oven and sprinkle over the arugula and pomegranate. Drizzle with a good glug of olive oil and eat straightaway.

ROASTED EGGPLANT, PESTO, AND TOMATO PIZZA

PESTO

- 1¼ cups (150 g) Brazil nuts
- ¼ cup (60 g) nutritional yeast flakes
- Generous 4 cups (100 g) fresh basil leaves
- 7 tablespoons (100 g) extra virgin olive oil
- Juice of 1 lemon
- Salt and freshly ground black pepper

Place the Brazil nuts and nutritional yeast in a food processor and whizz until finely chopped. Add the basil, oil, lemon juice, and salt and pepper and pulse a few more times.

- 1 eggplant, sliced
- ¼ cup (60 g) Tomato Sauce (page 113)
- 2 tablespoons (25 g) Pesto (above)
- Extra virgin olive oil, for drizzling

1. Preheat the oven to 475°F and place two flat baking sheets or pizza stones on the middle shelf to heat up.
2. Place two of the dough balls on a sheet of parchment paper. This makes transferring them to the oven easier. Roll them out to your desired size.
3. Lightly pan-fry the eggplant slices until just cooked.
4. Spread the tomato sauce onto the pizza bases, top with the eggplant, then drizzle over the pesto.
5. Bake in the oven for 10 to 12 minutes, keeping an eye on the crust.
6. Remove, drizzle with olive oil, and serve. Add more pesto if desired!

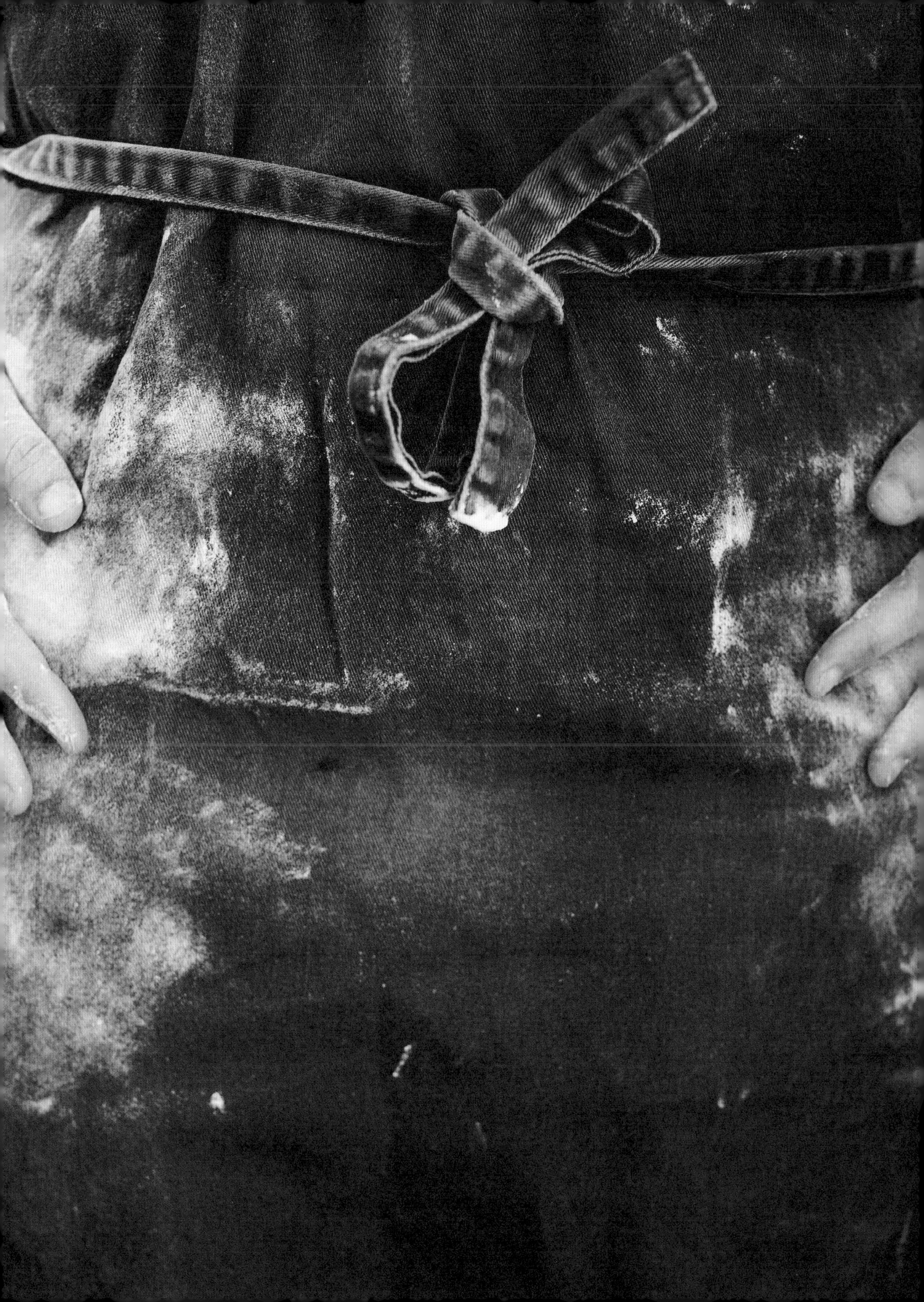

Cakes

Before I became ill I discovered a fabulous, quirky recipe for a carrot and olive oil cake. That same recipe later helped to change my life.

My constant quest for recipes began as a displacement activity. For many people with eating disorders, cooking well for others distracts from the turmoil inside their heads. And the better the food, the better the decoy. Over time the discipline became an ingrained skill, like music practice or times tables. For the last ten years I must have scanned at least 100 recipes a week. No glossy magazine, weekend supplement, or significant cookbook was safe: I'd tear out pages or tag them, adding to my trove of recipes.

I would dutifully cook them to the ounce. Leo jokingly offered me a white lab coat, but that discipline gave me a fantastic grounding and appreciation of ingredients, combinations, temperatures, different ovens, utensils, and pans.

After my illness, when I had finally seen for myself that it's not how much you eat that makes you fat or not (and that exercise alone is an inefficient tool for weight loss), I started to become much more creative in the kitchen.

So, back to the carrot and olive oil cake. Every time I had made it in the past to the recipe, people had loved it—me too. It was moist, didn't taste of carrot, and every mouthful was a treat. Logically, I thought I could never make it again, as it contained loads of ingredients I had committed to avoid. However, one day, I did something I had never done before—I went off recipe!

I halved the quantity of sugar and used a natural, low–glycemic index, organic coconut sugar instead. I switched to organic spelt flour and topped the cake with a homemade cashew nut frosting (another breakthrough recipe found in an anticancer book that's become a staple). I couldn't believe the outcome. The cake was (amazingly) even more delicious and the novelty of using interesting ingredients, and healthy ones at that, took my cooking pleasure to completely new heights. I was hooked. My friends couldn't stop talking about it.

We didn't realize at the time, but we'd just created the Modern Baker proposition of provenance, nutrition, and taste. This newfound, nonmedicated sense of well-being and happiness slowly grew into an urge to bake commercially. I wanted to share it with other people, especially those who'd been through a similar experience. Lindsay was the first person I had come across who perfectly understood what I was explaining and, because of her understanding of the science, she was full of ideas to perfect this type of healthy baking.

All the recipes in this section are based on exactly the same principles of lower, natural sugar levels and high-quality natural ingredients, sometimes with a sourdough starter, and liberally using fresh seasonal vegetables and fruits whenever possible.

My life-changer is the first recipe in this section, so you can find out for yourself just how revolutionary it can be. At the very least you'll enjoy an indulgent cake made entirely from healthy ingredients. Surely that's all up-side!

MELISSA'S LIFE-CHANGING CARROT AND OLIVE OIL CAKE

MAKES 1 × 9-inch round cake **EQUIPMENT** 9-inch round springform pan **DF**

≡

Sorry for the melodramatic title of this cake but to be honest it was life-changing for me, so please just go with it.

It's the complex play of the spices that really brings this cake to life. Cloves, cardamom, and cinnamon combine to heighten the flavors and aromas to an almost intoxicating level. With 3¾ cups of grated carrot in this cake there's no getting away from its presence, though it's surprising how the cake doesn't really taste of it. Its purpose is to bind in the flour—in this case spelt, which is higher in protein and fiber than wheat. The fruity olive oil unifies all the other flavors.

This recipe is so forgiving. Even overcooked, it's still moist and delicious!

- Scant 1 cup (215 g) extra virgin olive oil
- 1¼ cups (packed) (250 g) coconut sugar
- 4 large (220 g) eggs, beaten
- 1¾ cups (250 g) spelt flour
- 2 teaspoons (10 g) baking soda
- 2 teaspoons (10 g) baking powder
- 2 teaspoons (10 g) ground cinnamon
- 1 teaspoon (5 g) ground cloves
- 1 teaspoon (5 g) ground cardamom
- 1 teaspoon (5 g) salt
- 1 cup (12 5 g) pecans, coarsely chopped
- 3¾ cups (500 g) grated carrots
- Vanilla Cashew Nut Frosting or Maple Cream Cheese Frosting (pages 214 and 216)
- Coarsely chopped walnuts, for topping

1. Preheat the oven to 375°F and line a 9-inch round springform pan with parchment paper.

2. In a bowl, mix together the olive oil, sugar, and eggs until well combined.

3. In a second bowl, combine the flour and the other dry ingredients and make a well in the center. Add the egg and oil mixture and stir thoroughly until it is all blended. Finally, add the pecans and carrots and mix again.

4. Pour the batter into the pan and bake for about 1 hour 20 minutes, until a skewer inserted into the middle comes out clean.

5. Let the cake cool in the pan for 10 to 15 minutes, then turn it out onto a wire rack. Once it's completely cool, top it with either Vanilla Cashew Nut Frosting or Maple Cream Cheese Frosting.

NUTRITION NOTE

The olive oil is rich in monounsaturated fats that are better for your heart than the saturated fats in butter.

THE BIG CAKE

MAKES 1 × 8-inch round cake

EQUIPMENT 8-inch round springform pan

In the bakery we call this the "big cake" because it produces a cake that's deliciously light and airy, and looks really impressive crowned with different fruit toppings. It's a great base for an infinite variety of combinations; I've suggested some of our favorites, but the only limit is your own creativity.

We use quite a deep pan, so if you only have shallow ones you can divide the batter between two and bake for a shorter time, about 25 minutes, until a skewer comes out clean. It won't technically be a big cake anymore, but it will still taste as good.

- 5 large (275 g) eggs, separated
- Generous 1 cup (2¼ sticks/250 g) unsalted butter, at room temperature
- ¾ cup (200 g) honey or other liquid sweetener, such as maple or date syrup
- 1 teaspoon (5 g) vanilla extract
- Scant 1½ cups (190 g) all-purpose flour (spelt is good, or a good-quality gluten-free mix)
- 1¼ cups (120 g) almond meal
- 2 teaspoons (10 g) baking powder
- Spices and fruit of your choice (Variations on the following pages)

1. Preheat the oven to 400°F and line an 8-inch round springform pan with parchment paper.

2. In a bowl, beat the egg whites to stiff peaks with electric beaters.

3. In a second bowl, beat together the egg yolks, butter, honey, and vanilla until smooth and light. Add the flour, almond meal, baking powder, and spices, if using, and beat again until everything is incorporated.

4. Briskly mix in a third of the egg whites to loosen the mix, then gently fold in the remaining two-thirds, maintaining as much air as possible. Now carefully fold in two-thirds of your chosen fruit, if using.

5. Pour the batter into the pan and top with the rest of the fruit, if using. Bake in the oven for around 50 minutes, until a skewer inserted into the middle of the cake comes out clean.

6. Let cool in the pan for 10 to 15 minutes and then turn out onto a wire rack.

TURMERIC AND ORANGE BIG CAKE

≡

Turmeric and orange work wonderfully well together. The natural sweetness of the orange smooths out the punch of the turmeric, as well as adding some vitamin C. Add honey and this becomes a great cake to have in colds season.

It's terrific with our Yogurt Frosting (page 218)—and why not add the zest of an orange to the frosting for an extra citrus hit?

- Zest and juice of 2 oranges
- 1 teaspoon (5 g) ground turmeric
- ½ teaspoon (2.5 g) ground black pepper
- 1 teaspoon (5 g) honey

1 Add the orange zest to the cake batter with the butter and honey in Step 3. Mix the turmeric and black pepper in with the flour and almond meal.

2 Add the orange juice and 1 teaspoon honey to a small pan and cook over gentle heat for 10 to 15 minutes while the cake is in the oven. Pour this over the cake as soon as it comes out of the oven in Step 6, then let it cool completely in the pan.

NUTRITION NOTE

Using lemon with green tea has been shown to make catechins, a heart-healthy antioxidant, more bioavailable to the body.

MATCHA AND LEMON BIG CAKE

≡

You'll find matcha green tea powder making frequent appearances in this book, as it does in our store. It's a wonderful ingredient, not only for its vivid green coloring qualities but also for its famed healthiness.

- Zest and juice of 2 lemons
- 1 tablespoon (15 g) matcha green tea powder
- 1 teaspoon (5 g) honey

1 Add the lemon zest to the cake batter with the butter and honey in Step 3. Add the matcha powder in with the flour and almond meal.

2 Mix the lemon juice with the 1 teaspoon honey and pour over the cake as soon as it comes out of the oven. Let cool completely in the pan.

VARIATION

APPLE, ROSE, AND WALNUT BIG CAKE

Rose water brings out a deliciously exotic taste in the apples, but be careful not to use too much or it will feel like you are eating perfume. The walnuts here really add another layer to the diverse flavors of the cake.

- ¼ teaspoon (1 g) rose water
- 1¼ cups (120 g) ground walnuts
- 1 apple, unpeeled, cored, and finely chopped
- 1 apple, cored and sliced
- Chopped walnuts, for topping

1. Add the rose water to the cake batter with the honey and butter in Step 3. Replace the almond meal in the recipe with the ground walnuts. Fold the chopped apples through the cake batter just before it goes into the pan.

2. Top the cake with the sliced apple and chopped walnuts before you bake it.

NUTRITION NOTE

Rose water's health benefits have been believed and practiced for millennia in central Europe and the Middle East. Trials are under way to quantify its antioxidant properties.

VARIATION

STRAWBERRY AND PINK PEPPERCORN BIG CAKE

Pink peppercorns have a sweet and spicy flavor that is a lot more fragrant than black pepper. It pairs really well with the sweetness of the strawberries.

- ⅔ cup (200 g) date syrup
- 1 teaspoon (5 g) freshly ground pink peppercorns
- 1 cup (150 g) fresh strawberries, chopped

1. Replace the honey in the main cake recipe with the date syrup. Add the pink peppercorns with the flour and almond meal.

2. Fold half of the strawberries into the cake batter and use the rest to top the cake before you bake it.

NUTRITION NOTE

Like black pepper, pink peppercorns are believed to have antibacterial properties that can help fight colds and infections.

VARIATION

LIME, CHILE, AND CINNAMON BIG CAKE

This cake is for the adventurous. It started life as an experiment with some leftover ingredients and a hunch, and the result was great. The Asian-style flavors blend surprisingly well with the honey and the almonds.

- Zest and juice of 3 limes
- ½ teaspoon (2.5 g) fresh chile, minced
- ½ teaspoon (2.5 g) ground cinnamon
- 1 teaspoon (5 g) honey

1. Add the lime zest to the cake batter with the honey and butter in Step 3. Mix the chile and cinnamon in with the flour and almond meal.

2. Add the 1 teaspoon honey to the lime juice and pour over the cake as soon as it comes out of the oven. Let cool completely in the pan.

NUTRITION NOTE

Vitamin C helps to keep our immune system, bones, skin, teeth, and nervous system healthy. It also contributes to the reduction of tiredness and fatigue.

MODERN BAKER VICTORIA SPONGE

MAKES 1 × 8-inch round cake **EQUIPMENT** 8-inch round springform pan **GF** **DF**

The Victoria sponge is one of those absolutely classic cakes that is a staple of afternoon tea, cake stalls, and home baking everywhere. We wanted to create our own take on it, without refined sugar and using a combination of almond meal and buckwheat flour instead of all-purpose white flour. In the making it ended up both gluten-free and dairy-free as well, without any compromise on taste.

For the filling we use Raspberry Chia Jam (page 219), which is light and fresh, and so quick and easy to make. The result is a cake that retains the simplicity of the original Victoria sponge, but with a Modern Baker healthier twist—this is a very clean cake, full of goodness!

- 1 cup (200 g) coconut oil, melted
- Scant 1 cup (packed) (175 g) coconut sugar
- 4 large (220 g) eggs
- 1 teaspoon (5 g) vanilla extract
- Scant 1 cup (100 g) buckwheat flour
- 1 cup (100 g) almond meal
- 1 teaspoon (5 g) baking powder
- ½ teaspoon (5 g) baking soda
- Pinch (0.25 g) of salt

TO FILL

- Raspberry Chia Jam (page 219)
- Freeze-dried raspberry powder, for sprinkling (optional)

1. Preheat the oven to 400°F and line an 8-inch round springform pan with parchment paper.

2. In a bowl, combine the melted oil with the sugar, eggs, and vanilla.

3. In another bowl, mix together the flour, almond meal, baking powder, baking soda, and salt.

4. Add the dry ingredients to the wet ingredients and mix well until there are no dry patches.

5. Pour the batter into the pan and bake for 30 minutes, or until a skewer inserted into the middle comes out clean.

6. Let the cake cool in the pan for around 10 minutes and then turn out onto a wire rack. Once it's completely cool, slice it in half horizontally and fill with chia jam. Sprinkle the top with the raspberry powder, if desired.

NUTRITION NOTE

Not only is buckwheat flour GF, but it also contains protein and fiber, which are great for digestion.

CHOCOLATE MORINGA CAKE

≡

This chocolate cake makes everyone happy—health buffs, superfood skeptics, fans of pure indulgence.

Moringa is a small tree native to northern India, also known as the drumstick tree. Its leaves are packed with vitamins, minerals, and powerful antioxidants, long used in traditional medicine. You can buy the leaves dried in powdered form.

We like to top this cake with either our Vanilla Cashew Nut Frosting (page 214) or our Chocolate Cream Cheese Frosting (page 218).

This recipe makes a very large cake, so if you only have shallow pans divide the batter between two and bake for a shorter time, about 30 minutes, or until a skewer comes out clean.

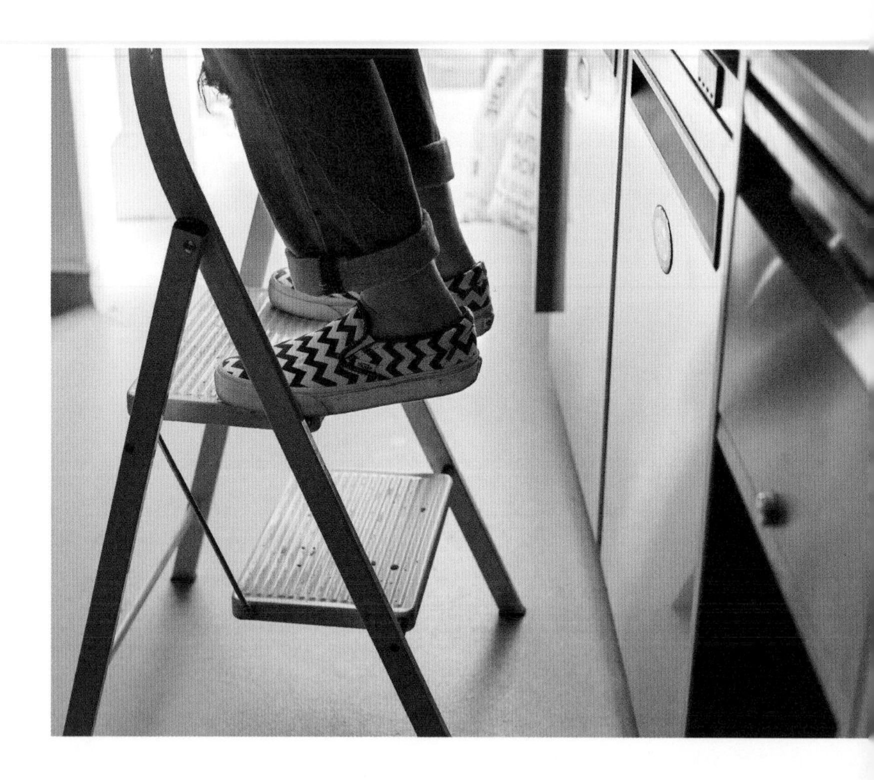

MAKES 1 × 8-inch round cake

EQUIPMENT 8-inch round springform pan and a balloon whisk

- ⅔ cup (150 g) whole Greek yogurt
- 1 cup (225 g) whole milk
- ½ cup (100 g) coconut oil, melted
- 2 teaspoons (10 g) vanilla extract
- 7 tablespoons (100 g) boiling water
- 1 cup (packed) (200 g) coconut sugar
- 2 tablespoons (25 g) lucuma powder
- Scant 2½ cups (325 g) spelt flour
- 1 cup (100 g) raw cacao powder
- 1 tablespoon (15 g) moringa powder
- 2 teaspoons (10 g) baking powder
- 1 teaspoon (5 g) baking soda
- Pinch (0.25 g) of salt

1. Preheat the oven to 400°F and line an 8-inch round springform pan with parchment paper.

2. In a bowl, combine the yogurt, milk, oil, and vanilla. Add the boiling water and mix together well.

3. In another bowl, briefly whisk together the sugar, lucuma, flour, cacao powder, moringa powder, baking powder, baking soda, and salt with a balloon whisk, to remove any lumps and incorporate some air.

4. Add the dry ingredients to the wet ingredients and mix well until it forms a smooth batter.

5. Pour the batter into the pan and bake for around 50 minutes, or until a skewer inserted in the middle comes out clean.

6. Let cool in the pan for 10 to 15 minutes, then turn out onto a wire rack. If frosting, frost once the cake is completely cool.

NUTRITION NOTE

Moringa is an excellent source of vitamins A and K and iron and contains protein, vitamin E, magnesium, and calcium. These help to keep your immune system, skin, and nervous system healthy and help to combat fatigue.

MACA AND VANILLA CAKE

≡

Customers often request a birthday cake for someone with dietary restrictions. We love this kind of challenge, as it gives us another excuse to experiment. On this occasion the customer wanted a birthday cake that was dairy-free and vegan and we topped it with our Vanilla Cashew Nut Frosting (page 214) and finished it off with raspberries, blueberries, and a few leaves of fresh mint. It was such a success that it's become part of our repertoire.

As for maca, it's a powerful Peruvian root with an earthy, nutty taste and a hint of butterscotch. Its powder is essentially a flour, but with the spelt taking that role it's here for its sweet, nutty contribution and amazing nutritional qualities. It also combines very well with the maple syrup and vanilla flavors.

- 1¾ cups (225 g) spelt flour
- 4 teaspoons (20 g) maca powder, plus more for dusting
- 1 teaspoon (5 g) baking powder
- 1 teaspoon (5 g) baking soda
- Pinch (0.25 g) of salt
- 1 cup (200 g) maple syrup
- ½ cup (100 g) coconut oil, melted
- 1 tablespoon (15 g) vanilla extract
- 1 tablespoon (15 g) apple cider vinegar
- ½ cup (120 g) warm water (it is important that the water is warm not cold, or it will turn the coconut oil solid)
- Vanilla Cashew Nut Frosting (page 214)

1. Preheat the oven to 400°F and line an 8-inch round springform pan with parchment paper.
2. In a bowl, mix the spelt flour, maca powder, baking powder, baking soda, and salt.
3. In another bowl, mix together the maple syrup, oil, vanilla, vinegar, and warm water.
4. Add the dry ingredients to the wet ingredients and whisk together well to remove any lumps.
5. Pour the mixture into the pan and bake for 40 minutes, or until a skewer inserted into the middle comes out clean.
6. Cool in the pan for 10 minutes, then turn out onto a wire rack.
7. When completely cool, top with the Vanilla Cashew Nut Frosting and a dusting of maca powder or some fresh fruit.

NUTRITION NOTE

Maca is thought of as a superfood. It is believed to give you energy and endurance. It's also used to improve hormonal balance.

MAKES 1 × 8-inch round cake **EQUIPMENT** 8-inch round springform pan **DF V+**

TANGY BARBERRY CAKE

MAKES 1 × 8-inch round cake **EQUIPMENT** 8-inch round springform pan **GF DF V+**

When you run a café with discerning and loyal customers, it's not only the best sellers that earn a devoted following. As anyone who is gluten-free knows, the pleasure of finding bread or cakes that taste good is worth any amount of effort—and once found, never forgotten.

So while this doesn't have the impact of a celebration cake, it has a special mystique thanks to the dried barberries—a fantastic find. I saw them being heralded as one of the new health foods on the block, so we thought we'd give them a go.

Once popular, barberries are now mainly found in Iranian regional cooking. They have a really zingy, sharp flavor that bursts in your mouth, so they can also be used as an alternative to citrus peel. They're not dissimilar from dried goji berries, so if you can't find them use goji berries instead.

NUTRITION NOTE

Barberries have similar health properties to gojis. They contain berberine, which can be anti-inflammatory and enhance the immune system.

- ½ cup (60 g) tapioca flour
- ½ cup (60 g) buckwheat flour
- 2 tablespoons (25 g) cornstarch
- Scant ½ cup (40 g) almond meal
- ¾ cup (packed) (150 g) coconut sugar
- 1½ teaspoons (7.5 g) baking powder
- 1 teaspoon (5 g) ground cinnamon
- Pinch (0.25 g) of salt
- ⅓ cup (50 g) dried barberries, soaked in ¼ cup (60 g) water for at least 10 minutes
- 2 tablespoons ground flaxseed, mixed with ¾ cup (180 g) almond milk for at least 10 minutes (it will form a loose paste)
- ½ cup (110 g) coconut oil, melted
- 1 teaspoon (5 g) vanilla extract
- Slivered almonds, for topping

1. Preheat the oven to 400°F and line an 8-inch round springform pan with parchment paper.
2. In a bowl, mix together the flours, cornstarch, almond meal, sugar, baking powder, cinnamon, and salt.
3. In another bowl, combine the barberries and their soaking water, the ground flaxseed and almond milk mix, oil, and vanilla.
4. Add the wet ingredients to the dry ingredients and combine them well. The mix will be quite wet.
5. Pour it into the prepared pan and top with the slivered almonds.
6. Bake for 30 to 40 minutes until a skewer inserted into the middle comes out clean. Let the cake cool in the pan for 10 minutes, then turn it out onto a wire rack.

SWEET POTATO AND BANANA FLOUR CAKE

MAKES 1 × 8-inch round cake

EQUIPMENT 8-inch round springform pan and a food processor

GF DF

I was excited when I read about banana flour in a Sunday newspaper. I immediately bought some for Lindsay, who of course started experimenting.

Banana flour is made from milled unripe bananas, generally from Brazil, and it's an excellent gluten-free ingredient—and doesn't taste of bananas. When combined with a small amount of fat, the beneficial beta-carotene antioxidants in sweet potato are significantly increased. The natural sweetness from the potato enables us to cut down on the added sugar.

If you can't find banana flour you could replace it with 1 cup of buckwheat flour.

- 10½ ounces (300 g) sweet potatoes
- 2 large (110 g) eggs
- ½ cup (packed) (100 g) coconut sugar
- ½ cup (120 g) almond milk
- ¼ cup (45 g) coconut oil, melted
- 1 teaspoon (5 g) vanilla extract
- Generous ¾ cup (90 g) banana flour
- ¼ cup (30 g) brown rice flour
- ⅓ cup (30 g) oats
- ¼ cup (30 g) ground flaxseed
- 1 teaspoon (5 g) ground cinnamon
- 1 teaspoon (5 g) mixed spice (page 144)
- 1½ teaspoons (7.5 g) baking powder
- Pinch (0.25 g) of salt

FOR THE CRUMBLE TOPPING

- 2 tablespoons (25 g) coconut oil
- 4 teaspoons (20 g) coconut sugar
- ⅓ cup (30 g)oats
- 2⅓ tablespoons (20 g) banana flour
- ½ teaspoon (2.5 g) ground cinnamon

1. Preheat the oven to 400°F and line an 8-inch round springform pan with parchment paper.
2. In a roasting pan, bake the sweet potatoes in their skins until they are soft. This should take 30 to 45 minutes. Peel and blitz in the food processor until smooth. Alternatively, peel and chop the sweet potatoes and boil in a pan for 20 minutes until soft. Blitz in a food processor until smooth. Let cool.
3. In a bowl, rub together the ingredients for the crumble topping and set to one side.
4. In another bowl, beat together the eggs, sweet potato puree, sugar, milk, oil, and vanilla.
5. In another bowl, stir together the banana flour, brown rice flour, oats, ground flaxseed, cinnamon, mixed spice, baking powder, and salt.
6. Add the dry ingredients to the wet ingredients and mix well.
7. Pour the batter into the prepared pan, smooth it over, and top with the crumble topping.
8. Bake for 30 to 40 minutes until a skewer inserted into the middle comes out clean. Let cool in the pan for 10 to 15 minutes and then turn out onto a wire rack.

NUTRITION NOTE

The banana flour is high in potassium and contains a resistant starch, a type of fiber. Sweet potatoes are packed with vitamins and minerals, including beta-carotene.

modernbaker

COFFEE AND PECAN NUT CAKE

MAKES 1 × 8-inch round cake

EQUIPMENT 2 × 8-inch round springform pans and a food processor

≡

From the start we knew we were going to care a lot about our coffee, and that provenance and taste mattered.

After much sampling we turned to the long-established, London-based Monmouth with its darker roast and bitter chocolate notes. Cue a coffee cake!

Coffee is one of the most heavily treated crops in the world, and the residues of pesticides and fertilizers actually make it harder for your body to access its beneficial antioxidants, so do use organic if you can.

- ½ cup (50 g) chopped pecans
- Scant 2 cups (packed) (170 g) coconut sugar
- 1 cup (2 sticks/225 g) unsalted butter
- 1½ cups (200 g) spelt flour
- 2½ teaspoons (12.5 g) baking powder
- ½ teaspoon (2.5 g) baking soda
- 4 extra-large (240 g) eggs
- 5 tablespoons (75 g) espresso, brewed and cooled (or cafetière coffee)
- Coffee Cream Cheese Frosting (page 216)
- 10 whole pecans, for decoration

1. Preheat the oven to 400°F and line two 8-inch round springform pans with parchment paper.

2. Put the chopped pecans and sugar into a food processor and blitz to a fine powder. Add the butter, flour, baking powder, baking soda, eggs, and coffee and mix to a smooth batter.

3. Divide the mixture between the two pans and bake in the oven for 25 minutes until the sponges have risen and feel springy to the touch. Let cool in the pan for 10 minutes and then turn out carefully onto a wire rack.

4. When the cakes are completely cool, sandwich the two halves with the Coffee Cream Cheese Frosting and top with the same. Finally, decorate the cake with the whole pecans.

NUTRITION NOTE

Did you know that organic coffee can actually be good for gut health? Its particular nutrients help diversify your intestinal bacteria. Adding a buttery flavor to a cake, the pecans are packed with health-benefiting minerals such as manganese, which helps to protect our bodies' cells from damage, and antioxidants.

ORCHARD CAKE

≡

As the name suggests, you can use whatever fruit comes to hand, even if it's slightly old. Grated fruit makes this cake incredibly moist, and also acts as a binding agent in place of eggs—a great tip for vegans.

You can enjoy it on its own with a cup of tea or as a great dessert, or top it with our Maple Cream Cheese Frosting (page 216).

I always have slices of this cake tucked away in the freezer at home, not only because it's so versatile but also because it's a great standby for friends with intolerances.

To make your own mixed spice, mix together equal amounts of ground cinnamon, allspice, ground ginger, ground nutmeg, and ground cloves. I recommend making a larger batch, combining 30g of each spice, and storing in a jar for use in multiple recipes.

- 2 eating or cooking apples, cored and grated
- 1 pear, cored and grated
- Scant 1 cup (180 g) coconut oil, melted
- ½ cup (150 g) maple syrup
- 1 teaspoon (5 g) vanilla extract
- Generous ¾ cup (100 g) buckwheat flour
- Generous 1¾ cups (180 g) almond meal
- ½ teaspoon (2.5 g) ground ginger
- ½ teaspoon (2.5 g) mixed spice (see left)
- 2 teaspoons (10 g) baking powder

1. Preheat the oven to 400°F and line an 8-inch round springform pan with parchment paper.
2. In a bowl, mix the grated apples and pear with the oil, maple syrup, and vanilla.
3. In another bowl, combine the flour, almond meal, spices, and baking powder.
4. Add the dry ingredients to the wet ingredients and mix until they are well combined.
5. Pour the mixture into the pan and bake for 40 to 50 minutes until a skewer inserted into the middle comes out clean. Let the cake cool in the pan for 10 minutes, then turn out onto a wire rack.

NUTRITION NOTE

Despite its name, buckwheat flour is ideal for those wishing to avoid wheat as it doesn't contain any! Bizarrely, it's related to the rhubarb family and contains minerals such as manganese, which is needed for a healthy nervous system.

MAKES 1 × 8-inch round cake **EQUIPMENT** 2 × 8-inch round springform pan **GF DF V+**

COFFEE, CHOCOLATE, AND CHESTNUT CAKE

MAKES 1 × 8-inch round cake
EQUIPMENT 8-inch round, deep springform pan
GF

≡

This is a really rich, indulgent cake, and the alliteration in the name seems to underline this—it just sounds so luscious!

Chestnut flour is interesting to work with. It's made from ground chestnuts and is naturally sweet, so you don't need to add as much sugar, but it does need more liquid so don't be worried by the seemingly large ratio of wet to dry ingredients here. The coffee acts as a lovely balance to the sweetness of chestnut and cacao.

- 3 large (165 g) eggs
- ¼ cup (packed) (50 g) coconut sugar
- 5 tablespoons (75 g) espresso, brewed and cooled (or cafetière coffee)
- 2 teaspoons (10 g) vanilla extract
- ½ cup (120 g) Greek yogurt, plus more for serving
- ⅔ cup (60 g) chestnut flour
- ⅓ cup (30 g) raw cacao powder
- ¼ cup (30 g) hemp protein powder
- 2 teaspoons (10 g) baking powder

1 Preheat the oven to 400°F and line an 8-inch round springform pan with parchment paper.

2 In a bowl, combine the eggs, sugar, espresso, vanilla, and yogurt and mix well.

3 In another bowl, stir together the flour, cacao, protein powder, and baking powder.

4 Add the dry ingredients to the wet ingredients and mix well. Pour the batter into the pan and bake for 30 to 35 minutes until a skewer inserted into the middle comes out clean.

5 Serve with more Greek yogurt.

NUTRITION NOTE

This cake is ideal for a sustained energy boost as the chestnut, hemp powder, and yogurt all add up to a useful protein hit.

CARROT, APPLE, AND WALNUT CAKE

MAKES 1 × 8-inch round cake

EQUIPMENT 8-inch round springform pan and a food processor

GF

We're not fans of complicated recipes, and although this one has quite a few ingredients, it's very easy to make and a good one for children to get involved with. The diverse ingredients mean there is lots to talk about, and it's a great way to learn about eating fruit and vegetables in new ways.

The grated apple and carrot make this cake very moist and naturally sweet, but if you want it a bit sweeter, just add a drop more maple syrup.

This cake makes a weekly appearance in the café and doesn't stay on the counter for very long, because it looks so indulgent! It's a great gluten-free option.

NUTRITION NOTE

Walnuts are a good source of the healthy fat alpha-linoleic acid (ALA), linked to a lower risk of heart disease in men and healthy bones, and of manganese and copper, which help to destroy free radicals.

- Scant 2 cups (160 g) grated carrot
- 1 apple, unpeeled, cored, and grated
- Scant 1 cup (180 g) coconut oil, melted
- ½ cup (150 g) maple syrup
- 2 large (110 g) eggs
- ¾ cup (100 g) walnuts, ground to a fine powder in a food processor
- ¾ cup (100 g) walnut halves, chopped, plus 10 more for topping
- Scant ½ cup (40 g) oats
- Scant ¾ cup (75 g) tapioca flour
- Scant ⅔ cup (75 g) buckwheat flour
- 2½ teaspoons (12.5 g) baking powder
- Pinch (0.25 g) of salt
- 2 teaspoons (10 g) ground cinnamon
- ½ teaspoon (2.5 g) ground nutmeg
- Maple Cream Cheese Frosting (page 216)

1. Preheat the oven to 400°F and line an 8-inch round springform pan with parchment paper.
2. In a large bowl, mix the grated carrot and apple with the oil, maple syrup, and eggs.
3. In another bowl, combine the ground walnuts, chopped walnut halves, oats, flours, baking powder, salt, and spices.
4. Add the dry ingredients to the wet ingredients and mix until completely combined.
5. Pour into the pan and bake for about 55 minutes until a skewer inserted into the middle comes out clean. Let cool in the pan for 10 minutes, then turn out carefully onto a wire rack.
6. Once it's cool we like to top this with our Maple Cream Cheese Frosting and a few extra walnut halves.

COMPLETELY COCONUT LOAF CAKE

MAKES 1 loaf **EQUIPMENT** 2-pound loaf pan **DF**

≡

I love the taste of coconut. Sometimes our palates like to have a hit that's driven by a single flavor. This cake was inspired by a brunch Lindsey was at where they served toasted coconut bread. Determined to include as much coconut as possible in her version, this delicious loaf cake is the result. It's really easy to make, with just seven ingredients. It's fabulous on its own, or topped with berries, coconut yogurt, and a drizzle of maple syrup. After a few days, it can be toasted and eaten with butter and coconut jam.

- 2 large (110 g) eggs
- 1¼ cups (300 g) coconut milk
- Generous ⅓ cup (75 g) coconut oil, melted
- ¾ cup (packed) (150 g) coconut sugar
- Generous 2¾ cups (370 g) spelt flour
- 2 teaspoons (10 g) baking powder
- 2 cups (150 g) dry unsweetened coconut, plus a little more for sprinkling on top
- Pinch (0.25 g) of salt

1. Preheat the oven to 400°F and line a 2-pound loaf pan with parchment paper.
2. In a bowl, mix together the eggs, milk, oil, and sugar.
3. In another bowl, combine the flour, baking powder, dry unsweetened coconut, and salt.
4. Add the dry ingredients to the wet ingredients and mix thoroughly. Pour into the prepared loaf pan and add some extra dry unsweetened coconut on top for decoration. Bake for 50 minutes until a skewer inserted in the middle comes out clean.
5. Let the cake cool in the pan for 10 to 15 minutes, then turn out onto a wire rack.

ZUCCHINI AND PECAN LOAF CAKE

≡

We have several keen gardeners among our customers, and luckily for us they often drop off their overflow produce at the bakery.

Zucchini seems to be particularly prone to a high-summer glut, and as a cake ingredient it brings a lovely moist texture. The lack of a flavor punch means you can play with other flavors around it.

Zucchini can hold a lot of water, which can affect the finished texture of the cake. If your grated zucchini seem very watery, place them in a clean cloth and wring out some of the liquid, then add them to the cake batter as normal.

The timing for cakes containing zucchini depend on their water content, so return the cake to the oven for another 10 minutes if it needs it. The skewer test works here.

We top this cake with our Maple Cream Cheese Frosting (page 216) but it's equally delicious without, or simply spread with some organic butter.

- 2 large (110 g) eggs
- ⅔ cup (150 g) extra virgin olive oil
- ⅔ cup (packed) (130 g) coconut sugar
- 2 cups (170 g) grated zucchini
- 1 teaspoon (5 g) vanilla extract
- 2 cups (270 g) spelt flour
- ½ teaspoon (2.5 g) baking soda
- ½ teaspoon (2.5 g) baking powder
- Pinch (0.25 g) of salt
- 1 teaspoon (5 g) ground cinnamon
- ½ cup (50 g) chopped pecans
- Maple Cream Cheese Frosting (page 216)

1 Preheat the oven to 400°F and line a 2-pound loaf pan with parchment paper.

2 In a bowl, beat together the eggs, olive oil, sugar, grated zucchini, and vanilla.

3 In another bowl, combine the flour, baking soda, baking powder, salt, cinnamon, and chopped pecans. By adding the nuts at this stage you coat them with flour, which helps to prevent them sinking to the bottom of the cake as it bakes.

4 Add the dry ingredients to the wet ingredients and mix well until thoroughly combined.

5 Pour into the loaf pan and bake in the oven for 50 minutes, or until a skewer inserted into the middle comes out clean.

6 Let cool in the pan for 10 to 15 minutes, then turn out onto a wire rack. Frost once the cake is completely cool.

NUTRITION NOTE

Zucchini are particularly high in fiber, which counteracts blood sugar surges and helps slow down digestion.

MAKES 1 loaf   **EQUIPMENT** 2-pound loaf pan

FIG UPSIDE-DOWN CAKE WITH LUCUMA

MAKES 1 × 8-inch round cake **EQUIPMENT** 8-inch round springform pan **GF** **DF**

Upside-down cake is so named because it's served that way from the baking pan, with the base upward. It's cooked with a layer of fruit on the bottom (which becomes the top), covered by a sponge.

Really it's more than just a cake—served warm with some coconut yogurt or cream on the side it becomes a fabulous dessert. You can make it with any fruit, so it's perfect for windfalls.

Here we've used figs because they go lovely and gooey in the oven without the need for any extra sugar. The fig season may be short, but this cake is so worth the wait.

- 4 to 5 figs, stems removed and cut in half
- ¾ cup (packed) (150 g) coconut sugar
- 2 tablespoons (25 g) lucuma powder
- 1 cup (200 g) coconut oil, melted
- 3 large (165 g) eggs, beaten
- 1 teaspoon (5 g) vanilla extract
- 1 teaspoon (5 g) ground cinnamon
- 1⅔ cups (150 g) chestnut flour
- ⅔ cup (75 g) buckwheat flour
- 2 tablespoons (25 g) almond milk
- 1½ teaspoons (7.5 g) baking powder

1. Preheat the oven to 400°F and line an 8-inch round springform pan with parchment paper.
2. Place the halved figs on the bottom of the pan, with the cut sides facing down. They should cover the bottom of the pan completely.
3. Mix all the other ingredients in a bowl, making sure that everything is well combined.
4. Carefully pour the batter over the figs, so you don't displace them.
5. Bake for 30 to 40 minutes until a skewer inserted into the middle of the cake comes out clean. Let the cake cool in the pan for at least 30 minutes, then turn it out onto a wire rack.

NUTRITION NOTE

Lucuma has a low GI value and the lower the GI, the slower the rise in blood sugar levels.

COCONUT AND LIME CAKE

≡

We created this cake the summer we opened, when we were dreaming of vacations as we worked by a hot oven! The creamy coconut and zesty lime combine to perfection. We love finishing off a cake with syrup while it's still hot, because it seeps into the cake and leaves it with a lovely sheen.

- 2 cups (250 g) spelt flour
- 2⅓ cups (175 g) dry unsweetened coconut, plus more for topping
- 1 tablespoon (15 g)baking powder
- ½ cup (150 g) maple syrup
- Scant 1 cup (200 g) coconut milk
- ½ teaspoon (2.5 g) vanilla extract
- Zest of 2 limes
- 2 large (110 g) eggs
- ¼ cup (50 g) coconut oil, melted
- Juice of 4 limes
- Scant ¼ cup (50 g) maple syrup

1. Preheat the oven to 400°F and line a 2-pound loaf pan with parchment paper.

2. In a bowl, mix together the spelt flour, dry unsweetened coconut, and baking powder.

3. In another bowl, combine the maple syrup, milk, vanilla, lime zest, eggs, and oil.

4. Add the dry ingredients to the wet ingredients and mix thoroughly. Pour into the pan and sprinkle with extra dry unsweetened coconut.

5. Bake for 40 minutes or until a skewer inserted into the middle comes out clean. Combine the lime juice with the maple syrup and pour over the cake while it is still hot, then let it cool completely in the pan before turning it out onto a wire rack.

MAKES 1 loaf **EQUIPMENT** 2-pound loaf pan **DF**

SIMNEL CAKE

MAKES 1 × 8-inch round cake **EQUIPMENT** 8-inch round springform pan

This Simnel cake goes down a treat in the lead-up to Easter. Apart from upgrading many of the ingredients for better health, our twist is the addition of goji berries and a few of our favorite spices. The use of dried berries and fruits adds chew and important fiber. Don't put too much on your plate—this is a rich one!

- ¾ cup (1½ sticks/175 g) unsalted butter
- Scant 1 cup (packed) (175 g) coconut sugar
- 3 large (165 g) eggs
- 1⅓ cups (175 g) spelt flour
- 1¼ cups (175 g) golden raisins
- ¾ cup (90 g) dried cranberries
- ¼ cup (30 g) dried goji berries
- Zest of 1 lemon, grated
- 2 teaspoons (10 g) baking powder
- 1 teaspoon (5 g) mixed spice (page 144)
- ½ teaspoon (2.5 g) ground turmeric
- ½ teaspoon (2.5 g) ground ginger
- ½ teaspoon (2.5 g) ground cinnamon
- ½ teaspoon (2.5 g) ground black pepper
- Pinch (0.25 g) of salt

FOR DECORATION

- Raw Marzipan (page 160)
- Honey or melted butter, for brushing
- Edible flowers, such as nasturtiums and violets

1. Preheat the oven to 325°F and line an 8-inch round springform pan with parchment paper.
2. Put all the ingredients into a large bowl. With electric beaters, beat them together until well combined.
3. Pour the batter into the prepared pan and smooth the top. Bake for 1½ to 2 hours until a skewer inserted into the middle comes out clean.
4. Let the cake cool in the pan for 10 minutes and then turn out onto a wire rack.
5. Once it's cool, use the pan as a template to cut out a round disk of raw marzipan.

→

6 Brush a little melted butter or honey over the top of the cake and lay the marzipan disk on top.

7 Use the remaining marzipan to make 11 equal-size balls to decorate the top of the cake. You can use honey to stick these on as well.

8 Top the cake with edible flowers such as nasturtiums and violets.

RAW MARZIPAN

GF DF V

Our raw marzipan is quick and easy to make, with the maple syrup helping to keep the delicious almond flavor. If you particularly like your marzipan, and I really do, you can also add a few drops of almond extract.

- Scant 3½ cups (340 g) almond meal
- 3 to 4 tablespoons (45 to 60 g) maple syrup
- 1 teaspoon (5 g) vanilla extract
- 2 to 3 drops of almond extract (optional)

1 Mix all the ingredients together to form a dough. Wrap in wax paper and chill until ready to use.

2 Roll out the dough between two sheets of parchment paper to ⅛ inch. You don't want to use flour to stop it sticking to the counter, and the paper will also make it easier to pick up.

APPLE AND ALMOND BUTTER CAKE

MAKES 1 × 8-inch round cake
EQUIPMENT 8-inch round springform pan
GF

Almonds and apples are cultivated in all temperate climates, so the marriage of them in a cake is inevitable—and they're a great mix. The apple skin is important, because as well as containing many of the nutrients it provides texture—always welcome in a cake.

The almond butter gives a really rich flavor, offset by the cinnamon. We use smooth almond butter but you could use the crunchy kind if that's more to your taste.

- 1 cup (200 g) coconut oil, melted and cooled
- 2 large (110 g) eggs
- 7 tablespoons (100 g) smooth almond butter
- 2 teaspoons (10 g) vanilla extract
- Scant 1 cup (packed) (175 g) coconut sugar, plus 1 tablespoon (15 g) for topping
- 1 cup (100 g) almond meal
- Generous 1 cup (150 g) spelt flour
- 2 teaspoons (10 g) baking powder
- 2 eating apples, unpeeled, cored, and chopped into small chunks (save ½ apple for topping)

1. Preheat the oven to 400°F and line an 8-inch round springform pan with parchment paper.

2. In a bowl, beat together by hand the oil, eggs, almond butter, and vanilla.

3. In another bowl, mix together the sugar, almond meal, flour, and baking powder. Toss the chopped apples through the dry mix—this will help to stop them from sinking to the bottom during the bake.

4. Pour the wet ingredients into the dry ingredients and mix well. Pour the batter into the pan, top with the reserved apple, sliced, and sprinkle with the tablespoon of sugar.

5. Bake for 30 to 40 minutes until a skewer inserted into the middle comes out clean. Let the cake cool in the pan for 10 minutes, then turn out onto a wire rack.

NUTRITION NOTE

Almonds are a significant source of protein, fiber, and healthy unsaturated fats, and an excellent source of vitamin E and magnesium.

BANANA, CINNAMON, AND LUCUMA CAKE

MAKES 1 loaf
EQUIPMENT 2-pound loaf pan
GF DF V+

We often get customers in the bakery asking for a cake suitable for vegans. This one is perfect because it's also absolutely delicious! It's gooey and indulgent, almost as much a dessert as it is a cake.

Lucuma starts life as a high-altitude, very dense tree fruit. It's harvested before it becomes soft, then left to lightly ferment before being dried and milled into a powder—it's rarely used in fruit form. Because it's so sweet, you need less of other sugars.

- 4 bananas, mashed
- ½ cup (110 g) coconut oil, melted
- ¾ cup (packed) (150 g) coconut sugar, plus more for topping
- 3 tablespoons (45 g) almond milk
- 1 teaspoon (5 g) vanilla extract
- 1 teaspoon (5 g) baking powder
- 2 teaspoons (10 g) ground cinnamon
- ½ teaspoon (2.5 g) baking soda
- 2¾ cups (275 g) almond meal
- 2 tablespoons (25 g) lucuma powder
- 1 banana, sliced lengthwise, for topping

1. Preheat the oven to 400°F and line a 2-pound loaf pan with parchment paper.
2. In a bowl, mix together the mashed bananas, oil, sugar, milk, and vanilla.
3. In another bowl, combine the baking powder, cinnamon, baking soda, almond meal, and lucuma powder.
4. Add the dry ingredients to the wet ingredients and mix well so that there are no dry patches remaining.
5. Pour into the prepared loaf pan and top with the sliced banana and a sprinkling of coconut sugar.
6. Bake for 55 minutes, or until a skewer inserted into the middle comes out clean. Let this cake cool completely in the pan as it can be quite delicate if taken out of the pan too early.

NUTRITION NOTE

Research has shown that cinnamon can lower blood sugar levels, among other health benefits.

PLUM, CHESTNUT, AND BLACK PEPPER CAKE

MAKES 1 × 8-inch round cake
EQUIPMENT 8-inch round springform pan
GF (if using gluten-free flour)

≡

The black pepper in this cake works really well with the sweetness of the plums and the earthiness of the chestnut flour. These spices make a refreshing change from the traditional winter double act of cinnamon and cloves. The turmeric's smokiness sits well with the black pepper's sharpness. All these combinations are definitely something we will be exploring further.

- 1½ cups (140 g) chestnut flour
- 1 cup (140 g) gluten-free all-purpose flour or spelt flour
- 2 teaspoons (10 g) baking powder
- 1 teaspoon (5 g) ground black pepper
- ¼ teaspoon (1 g) ground turmeric
- Pinch (0.25 g) of salt
- 10 tablespoons (1¼ sticks/140 g) butter
- Scant ¾ cup (packed) (140 g) coconut sugar, plus 1 tablespoon for topping
- 2 large (110 g) eggs
- 4 to 5 plums, pitted and cut into halves

1. Preheat the oven to 400°F and line an 8-inch round springform pan with parchment paper.

2. In a bowl, mix together the flours, baking powder, pepper, turmeric, and salt.

3. In another bowl, beat together using electric beaters the butter and sugar until light and fluffy. Beat in the eggs one at a time. Don't worry if the mix looks slightly curdled, this will all be resolved.

4. Beat the dry ingredients into the wet ingredients one-quarter at a time. Pour the batter into the pan, top with the halved plums, and sprinkle with sugar.

5. Bake for 40 minutes until a skewer inserted into comes out clean. Cool in the pan for 10 minutes, then turn out onto a wire rack.

→

NUTRITION NOTE

Turmeric is packed with health benefits, and combining it with black pepper is believed to make it easier to absorb into the body.

CHOCOLATE, AVOCADO, AND MILLET CAKE

MAKES 1 × 8-inch round cake

EQUIPMENT 8-inch round springform pan and a high-speed blender or food processor **GF DF**

This is the sort of ingredient combination that our customers expect from us, and it's why they come back. There's always plenty of discussion about this cake, and everyone wants to try it, especially the children. There's an air of excitement, with teaspoons for everyone to try a mouthful.

Who would have thought we'd be putting avocados in a cake! But why not? Their fat is healthier than butter, and they give a wonderful creamy texture. This is a decadent, fudgy cake and with some organic Greek yogurt it makes a fabulous dessert.

Unusually, we do suggest using a blender or processor for this one, as the avocado works best when it's really smooth.

- 2 ripe medium Hass avocados, peeled and pitted
- 2 cups (100 g) hulled millet grain (not flour)
- 1 cup (100 g) almond meal
- Scant ½ cup (50 g) buckwheat flour
- ½ cup (50 g) raw cacao powder
- ½ cup (150 g) maple syrup
- 1½ teaspoons (7.5 g) baking powder
- ½ teaspoon (2.5 g) baking soda
- 2 teaspoons (10 g) vanilla extract
- 7 tablespoons (100 g) almond milk
- Chocolate and Avocado Ganache (page 215)

1. Preheat the oven to 400°F and line an 8-inch round springform pan with parchment paper.

2. Place all the ingredients in a high-speed blender or a food processor. Blend until smooth and completely combined. The mixture can be quite stiff so you might need to scrape down the edges a few times.

3. Pour the mixture into the pan and bake in the oven for 30 to 40 minutes until a skewer inserted into the middle comes out clean.

4. Let the cake cool in the pan for 10 minutes, then turn out onto a wire rack.

5. To make this cake really indulgent, once it's cool top it with our Chocolate and Avocado Ganache.

NUTRITION NOTE

Millet is high in important nutrients, especially magnesium, and in fiber. As this recipe uses the whole grain, not the flour, it retains even more of these benefits.

APPLE AND SOURDOUGH BREAD PUDDING CAKE

MAKES 1 × 8-inch round cake
EQUIPMENT 8-inch round springform pan and a food processor

≡

This cake is a great way to use up leftover sourdough bread, and is our take on a traditional bread pudding (not to be confused with bread and butter pudding, which is about layering slices). Here we have simplified it, adding Greek yogurt to complement the sourdough taste and convert it from a cake into a dessert.

You can substitute any fruit or combination of fruits, throwing in some blackberries or switching to pears, for example.

- Generous 2 cups (500 g) Greek yogurt
- 3½ tablespoons (50 g) unsalted butter
- 2 large (110 g) eggs
- Scant 3½ cups (200 g) sourdough bread crumbs, made in a food processor (you can use whichever bread you have; we particularly like rye sourdough here)
- ½ cup (packed) (100 g) coconut sugar
- 2 apples, unpeeled, cored, and cut into chunks
- ⅔ cup (50 g) slivered almonds

1. Preheat the oven to 400°F and line an 8-inch round springform pan with parchment paper.
2. In a pan, bring the yogurt and butter gradually to a boil. Take off the heat and let cool until just warm. Add the eggs and mix in well.
3. In a bowl, mix together the bread crumbs, sugar, and apples.
4. Add the yogurt mix to the bread crumb mix and combine thoroughly. Pour the mixture into the pan and top with the slivered almonds.
5. Bake for 45 minutes until a deep golden brown. Let the cake cool in the pan for 10 minutes, then turn out onto a wire rack.

NUTRITION NOTE

With sourdough bread at its heart and live bacteria yogurt, this is a good example of how you can combine good digestive tract health and amazing taste in one!

PARSNIP AND COCONUT CAKE

MAKES 1 × 8-inch round cake
EQUIPMENT 8-inch round springform pan

≡

On a trip to New York, Lindsay was dining at a Michelin-star restaurant with parsnip cake on the menu. She was intrigued, and the second she arrived home she went straight to the kitchen and tried to make one herself.

Lindsay now recognizes that as the moment when she knew she wanted to experiment with different ingredients, especially ones with healthier properties.

In a similar way to carrots, the earthiness of parsnips works fantastically well with the maple syrup and helps keep the cake moist.

- About 11½ ounces (320 g) parsnips, peeled, cored, and coarsely grated
- Scant 1 cup (180 g) coconut oil, melted
- Scant ⅔ cup (180 g) maple syrup
- 3 large (165 g) eggs
- 1 teaspoon (5 g) vanilla extract
- Scant 1¼ cups (160 g) spelt flour
- 1⅓ cups (100 g) dry unsweetened coconut
- 2 teaspoons (10 g) baking powder
- 1 teaspoon (5 g) mixed spice (page 144)
- ½ teaspoon (2.5 g) ground ginger
- Maple Cream Cheese Frosting (page 216)

1. Preheat the oven to 400°F and line an 8-inch round springform pan with parchment paper.

2. In a bowl, combine the parsnips, oil, maple syrup, eggs, and vanilla.

3. In another bowl, mix together the flour, dry unsweetened coconut, baking powder, and spices.

4. Add the dry ingredients to the wet ingredients and mix well.

5. Pour the batter into the pan and bake for around 50 minutes, or until a skewer inserted into the middle comes out clean. Let cool in the pan for 10 minutes and then turn out carefully onto a wire rack.

6. Once it's cool, top with our Maple Cream Cheese Frosting. It's especially delicious if you stir some extra dry unsweetened coconut into the frosting.

NUTRITION NOTE

Parsnips are full of vitamins and minerals and high in fiber. Paired with spelt flour and dry unsweetened coconut, this packs a fibrous punch.

BREAKFAST FRIANDS

≡

Friands, or Friends as they are often accidentally called by many customers, are deliciously light little almond cakes, traditionally oval in shape.

Our fruity friands were an immediate hit with customers and we found that lots of people were buying them to have for breakfast. It made us wonder if there was a way we could make them slightly more substantial, and with more of the things you would traditionally associate with a muesli breakfast. We haven't specified the type of dried fruit to use as we like to use a combination of a few. Ideally, choose some you have not had in the past week to drive variety in your diet. If your dried fruit is large, such as figs or dates, chop it to fit.

Warm, with yogurt and a slice of fruit or a banana, these make the perfect breakfast.

You can get specialized friand pans, but if you can't get hold of one you can just use a muffin tray. Grease it well and only fill with about 1 heaping dessertspoon of the mix.

- Melted coconut oil, for greasing
- 1 cup (100 g) almond meal
- ¼ cup (35 g) chopped hazelnuts
- ⅓ cup (packed) (70 g) coconut sugar
- Scant ¼ cup (20 g) oats
- Scant ½ cup (50 g) mixed dried fruits (goji berries, cranberries, golden raisins, chopped dried apricots)
- ½ teaspoon (2.5 g) baking soda
- Pinch (0.25 g) of salt
- 3 large (165 g) eggs
- 1 teaspoon (5 g) vanilla extract

1. Preheat the oven to 375°F and grease nine holes of a muffin tray or friand pan liberally with the melted oil.

2. In a bowl, mix together the almond meal, chopped hazelnuts, sugar, oats, dried fruit, baking soda, and salt. Add the eggs and vanilla and mix well until thoroughly combined.

3. Divide the batter evenly among the nine greased holes.

4. Bake in the oven for 15 to 18 minutes until golden. Let cool in the pan for 10 minutes, then gently remove them. These are equally delicious warm from the pan or cool with a spoonful of Greek yogurt.

NUTRITION NOTE

A perfect little breakfast in two delicious mouthfuls. The oats and nuts give you plenty of fiber.

MAKES 9 friands **EQUIPMENT** 12-cup muffin tray or friand pan **GF** **DF**

FRUITY FRIANDS

MAKES 9 friands

EQUIPMENT 12-cup muffin tray or friand pan

GF DF

These are an absolute savior in the bakery, because they are quick to whip up on those days when we've had a run on cakes and need more really quickly. Don't tell anyone, but they can be made by any member of the staff, not just the bakers.

We top our fruity friands with whatever fresh fruit we have at hand; berries are good, blueberries and raspberries are particular favorites. If your seasonal fruit is bigger, chop to fit. You won't find a simpler baked treat.

These look cute too . . . perfectly formed little cakes.

- Melted coconut oil, for greasing
- 1⅓ cups (135 g) almond meal
- ½ teaspoon (2.5 g) baking soda
- Pinch (0.25 g) of salt
- ⅓ cup (packed) (70 g) coconut sugar
- 3 large (165 g) eggs
- Fruit, for topping

1 Preheat the oven to 375°F and grease nine holes of a friand pan or muffin tray liberally with the melted oil.

2 In a bowl, combine the almond meal, baking soda, salt, and sugar. Add the eggs and mix thoroughly.

3 Spoon the batter into the pan, about 1½ tablespoons per friand, and top with your choice of fruit. Make sure the fruit doesn't touch the pan as this will make the friands stick to it.

4 Bake for 15 to 18 minutes until golden, then let cool in the pan for 10 minutes before gently removing them.

NUTRITION NOTE

The almond meal not only sidesteps the gluten question for those avoiding that, but it's also a great way to pick up some protein.

CHOCOLATE AND PEAR SLICE

MAKES 8 slices
EQUIPMENT 10½ × 8-inch brownie tray
GF

☰

Pears are less acidic than their relative the apple, with a more honeyed taste, and their rich, aromatic flavor comes through the cooking process really well. There are many varieties of pear to choose from, but any one will do. As with many fruits, pears need the right flavor partners. The sweeter spices work particularly well, in this case cinnamon, and when combined with good-quality chocolate you have a flavor match made in heaven.

This recipe is for a flat cake, to cut into eight slices like a brownie. It makes a truly delicious, indulgent dessert.

- 7 tablespoons (100 g) unsalted butter
- 4 just-ripe pears, unpeeled, cored, and quartered
- 4 teaspoons (20 g) coconut sugar
- 1 teaspoon (5 g) ground cinnamon
- 5½ ounces (150 g) coconut sugar–sweetened chocolate
- 4 large (220 g) eggs
- ⅓ cup (packed) (60 g) coconut sugar blended with 1 tablespoon (15 g) cornstarch
- 2 tablespoons (25 g) chestnut flour

1. Preheat the oven to 400°F. Line a 10½ × 8-inch brownie tray with parchment paper.

2. In a pan, melt 1½ tablespoons of the butter and gently cook the pears with the butter, sugar, and cinnamon for 5 minutes until starting to soften, to let the flavors develop.

3. In a pan, melt the chocolate with the remaining butter over very gentle heat. Let cool.

4. In a bowl, combine the eggs with the sugar and cornstarch blend. Add the flour, mix well, and then add the melted chocolate.

5. Pour the mixture into the tray and top with the cooked pears. Bake for 15 to 20 minutes. Let cool, then cut into slices.

NUTRITION NOTE

You will retain more fiber by keeping the skin on your fruit and many of the nutrients, such as flavonoids, can be more concentrated in the skin of the pear.

Sourdough cinnamon bun
£2.20

MAPLE SUGAR AND BLUEBERRY SCONES

MAKES about 8 fairly large scones **EQUIPMENT** baking sheet and a round cutter

☰

This twist on the classic fruit scone is our alternative to the ubiquitous blueberry muffin. We think its harder and drier bite, along with spelt flour's natural nuttiness, makes it much more delicious.

We like making these quite big, and if you're entertaining, a combination of these and the matcha green tea ones together on a large cake plate looks stunning. There's always an air of excitement when they come out of the oven.

Maple sugar gives a subtle maple taste that goes perfectly with blueberries, a very North American combination. If you can't get hold of maple sugar you can replace it with 1 tablespoon of maple syrup or an equal quantity of coconut sugar.

— ⅓ cup (80 g) butter, at room temperature
— 3 cups (400 g) spelt flour
— 1 heaping tablespoon (30 g) baking powder
— ¼ cup (60 g) maple sugar
— Scant 1 cup (100 g) fresh or frozen blueberries
— Scant 1 cup (220 g) milk
— Beaten egg or milk, for glazing (optional)

1 Preheat the oven to 450°F and line a baking sheet with parchment paper.

2 In a large bowl, rub together the butter, flour, and baking powder, using a knife or your fingertips, until you get a texture like fine sand. Stir in the maple sugar and blueberries.

3 Add the milk and mix quickly, until the dough just comes together. It is important not to overwork the dough, as it will become stiff and won't rise as well during baking.

4 Turn out the dough onto a floured counter and pat it down until it is about 1 inch thick. Use a cutter to cut out circles, but be sure not to twist the cutter as you do so, as it will constrain the gluten and prevent the scones from rising as well.

5 Place the scones on the baking sheet. If you like a shiny top to your scones, brush them with some beaten egg or milk. Don't let the glaze drip down the sides of the scones, as this will make them lopsided.

6 Bake the scones for 20 minutes until turning golden brown. Transfer them to a wire rack as soon as they come out of the oven.

NUTRITION NOTE

The superfood qualities of blueberries are well known, focused mainly on their antioxidant levels (most strong-colored fruits and vegetables are high in these).

MATCHA GREEN TEA AND LEMON SCONES

MAKES about 8 fairly large scones
EQUIPMENT baking sheet and a round cutter

Every now and then the urge for a cream tea treat comes to us all. A nice big scone always has great visual impact, but when it's bright green and with the promise of a lemon bite, it challenges the senses and steals the show.

We like to eat these still warm from the oven, served with some of our lemon and honey curd and, for a really indulgent treat, some thick coconut yogurt.

- ⅓ cup (80 g) butter, at room temperature
- 3 cups (400 g) spelt flour
- 1 tablespoon (15 g) matcha green tea powder
- Grated zest of 1 lemon
- 1 heaping tablespoon (30 g) baking powder
- 3 tablespoons (packed) (45 g) coconut sugar
- Scant 1 cup whole milk
- Beaten egg or milk, for glazing (optional)

1. Preheat the oven to 450°F and line a baking sheet with parchment paper.
2. In a large bowl, rub together the butter, flour, matcha green tea powder, lemon zest, and baking powder using a knife or your fingertips until you get a texture like fine sand. Stir the sugar through.
3. Add the milk and mix quickly until the dough just comes together. It is important not to overwork the dough, as it will become stiff and won't rise as well during baking.
4. Turn out the dough onto a floured counter and pat it down until it is about 1 inch thick. Use a cutter to cut out circles, but be sure not to twist the cutter as you do so, as it will constrain the gluten and prevent the scones from rising as well.
5. Place the scones on the prepared baking sheet. If you like a shiny top to your scones, brush them with some beaten egg or milk. Don't let the glaze drip down the sides of the scones, as this will make them lopsided.
6. Bake the scones for 20 minutes until turning a green-tinged golden brown. Transfer them to a wire rack as soon as they come out of the oven.

NUTRITION NOTE

Matcha tea was long thought of as a magical elixir, and there's no doubt about the growing body of evidence supporting its benefits. It also combines perfectly with the citrus flavors.

QUINOA BROWNIES

≡

These brownies have the perfect gluten-free headline of being completely flourless and grain free—yet they are also a treat for everyone else. They are really easy to make, so they're another good one for making with children.

We think the ideal brownie should be slightly gooey in the middle, and not cakey at all. To achieve this perfection it's important not to overbake them. They should still have a bit of wobble when they come out of the oven.

The chocolate chips we use in this recipe are sweetened with coconut sugar, but you can use ordinary good-quality semisweet chocolate instead.

- 3½ ounces (100 g) coconut sugar–sweetened chocolate
- ½ cup (100 g) coconut oil
- ½ cup (120 g) almond butter
- 1¼ cups (230 g) cooked quinoa (⅔ cup/115 g raw quinoa cooked in water for about 20 minutes)
- ⅔ cup (60 g) raw cacao powder
- 2 large (110 g) eggs
- 2 teaspoons (10 g) vanilla extract
- ½ teaspoon (2.5 g) salt
- ¼ teaspoon (1 g) baking soda
- ½ cup (150 g) maple syrup

1. Preheat the oven to 400°F. Line a 10½ × 8-inch brownie tray with parchment paper.

2. Melt the chocolate over very gentle heat with the oil and almond butter.

3. Add all the ingredients (including the chocolate mix) to a food processor. Blend until well combined. The quinoa will break down slightly but not completely, which is what gives a really nice texture to the brownies.

4. Pour the batter into the prepared tray and smooth the top.

5. Bake for approximately 20 minutes; the brownies should still be slightly sticky when you take them out. Let cool in the pan and slice into eight equal portions.

NUTRITION NOTE

Quinoa is an uber-healthy edible seed. What has turned it into a wonder food in recent years are its GF properties and its presence of essential amino acids.

MAKES 8 brownies **EQUIPMENT** 10½ × 8-inch brownie tray and a food processor **GF** **DF**

SOURDOUGH CAKES

≡

The reason we use a sourdough starter in our bread is because it adds flavor, texture, and health qualities. So why wouldn't we use one in some of our cakes as well?

If we could achieve just one healthy baking result, it would be to get sourdough cakes accepted and understood for what they really have to offer baking. Like sourdough bread, these cakes do require a bit more preparation, but they are definitely worth any amount of extra planning because they take baking into a new dimension.

We have created our own special sweet starter, which is different from a bread starter in that it has a fruity, caramel flavor. As with the bread starter, you keep some of it back for your next cake. Once it's going, it is in theory yours forever, and unique to you.

SOURDOUGH CAKE SWEET STARTER

≡

Master this starter and you really have crossed the healthy baking line, but it isn't difficult. We use spelt flour and cow's milk, but for a gluten-free version simply use brown rice flour, and for plant-based use any dairy-free milk of your choice, such as oat, almond, or coconut.

EQUIPMENT

A container with a lid.

DAY 1

- 1 teaspoon (5 g) milk
- 1 teaspoon (5 g) spelt flour
- 1 teaspoon (5 g) coconut sugar

1. In a container with a lid, mix the milk, flour, and sugar. We recommend mixing with your hands rather than a spoon. We all have naturally occurring yeasts on our hands, so this can give your starter a real boost.

2. Leave the mixture overnight at room temperature. Cover it with the lid but do not make it airtight. A screw-top jar with the lid partly done up is perfect. You want the yeasts in the air to get in, but you also want to stop the mixture from drying out.

DAY 2

- Sweet starter made on Day 1
- 1 teaspoon (5 g) milk
- 1 teaspoon (5 g) spelt flour
- 1 teaspoon (5 g) coconut sugar

Discard half of your Day 1 mix and to what's left, add the milk, flour, and sugar. Leave at room temperature overnight as before.

DAYS 3 AND 4

Repeat Day 2.

DAY 5

1. By now your starter should be bubbling away. If it is not, continue to repeat Day 2 until it is. Once bubbling, top it off with the quantities required for your recipe and leave overnight.

2. Just like our bread starter, this keeps well in the refrigerator, so make sure you never use it all up on a recipe; always keep some behind for next time. And don't worry if it seems to have split when you take it out of the refrigerator; just give it a good stir and add your topping-off ingredients.

CHOCOLATE SOURDOUGH CAKE

MAKES 1 × 8-inch round cake **EQUIPMENT** 8-inch round springform pan

This cake is a universal favorite with our customers, our staff, and our families. More than one customer has said it is the best thing they have ever eaten!

We generally top it with our Chocolate Cashew Nut Frosting (page 214) and cacao nibs, often adding flowers for a celebratory touch. The cacao nibs are a gorgeous, unexpected crunch.

DAY 1

- 5 tablespoons (75 g) whole milk
- Generous ⅓ cup (75 g) (packed) coconut sugar
- ½ cup (75 g) spelt flour
- Active Sweet Starter (page 184)

Add the milk, sugar, and flour to the whole quantity of the Active Sweet Starter. Stir well and leave loosely covered at room temperature overnight.

DAY 2

- 8 ounces (225 g) recipe starter from Day 1
- Scant ½ cup (115 g) whole milk
- 2 large (110 g) eggs
- ½ cup (100 g) coconut oil, melted
- Scant ⅔ cup (120 g)(packed) coconut sugar
- 1 teaspoon (5 g) vanilla extract
- 1 cup (150 g) spelt flour
- Scant ½ cup (40 g) raw cacao powder
- 1 teaspoon (5 g) baking soda
- Pinch (0.25 g) of salt
- Chocolate Cashew Nut Frosting (page 214)

1. Preheat the oven to 400°F and line an 8-inch round springform pan with parchment paper.
2. In a large bowl, mix together the recipe starter, milk, eggs, oil, sugar, and vanilla.
3. In another bowl, whisk together the flour, cacao, baking soda, and salt. Whisking the ingredients has a similar effect to sifting, it incorporates air and also removes lumps from the flour and cacao.
4. Add the dry ingredients to the wet ingredients and beat together well.
5. Pour the batter into the pan and bake for 45 to 50 minutes until a skewer inserted in the middle comes out clean. Cool in the pan for 10 minutes and then turn out onto a wire rack. Once completely cool, frost with the Chocolate Cashew Nut Frosting.

NUTRITION NOTE

When a cocoa bean is processed, its health benefits are reduced. The pure, unadulterated cacao (the raw cocoa bean) is packed with antioxidants and it has been shown to help stimulate the production of endorphins that make you feel happy. It's the same effect we get after laughing, or exercising.

LEMON SOURDOUGH CAKE

≡

Citrus and sourdough work really well together. Any citrus will do, but lemon is always a winner. The secret to making these flavors combine so well in this cake is to make it more caramelly than you would normally expect in a lemon cake, which comes from the coconut sugar and spelt. Also, by adding the zest to the sourdough batter it becomes part of the body of the cake.

The cake is rich and flavorful in its own right, and strangely pleasant a few days old and slightly dry, but topped with our Lemon Cream Cheese Frosting (page 219) it becomes a sublime indulgence.

DAY 1

- Generous ⅓ cup (75 g) (packed) coconut sugar
- 5 tablespoons (75 g) whole milk
- ½ cup (75 g) spelt flour
- Active Sweet Starter (page 184)

Add the sugar, milk, and flour to the whole quantity of the sweet starter and mix well. Leave loosely covered at room temperature overnight.

DAY 2

- 8 ounces (225 g) recipe starter from Day 1
- Scant 2 cups (180 g) (packed) coconut sugar, plus 1 tablespoon for topping
- 2 large (110 g) eggs
- ½ cup (50 g) yogurt
- Scant 2 cups (180 g) coconut oil, melted
- Grated zest and juice of 2 lemons
- 1¾ cups (225 g) spelt flour
- 2 teaspoons (10 g) baking powder
- Pinch (0.25 g) of salt

1. Preheat the oven to 400°F and line an 8-inch round springform pan with parchment paper.
2. In a bowl, mix together the recipe starter, scant 2 cups (180 g) of the sugar, the eggs, yogurt, oil, and lemon zest.
3. In another bowl, whisk together the flour, baking powder, and salt. Add the dry ingredients to the wet ingredients and mix well.
4. Pour the batter into the pan and bake for 50 minutes, or until a skewer inserted into the middle comes out clean.
5. While the cake is baking, mix together the lemon juice and remaining sugar. Pour the juice over the cake while it is still warm from the oven. Let cool completely in the pan, as this will give the cake more time to absorb the lemon juice.

NUTRITION NOTE

As with most plants that we peel, the zest of a lemon has up to ten times more flavonoids than the juice, so it is worth using even in these small amounts.

MAKES 1 × 8-inch round cake **EQUIPMENT** 8-inch round springform pan

GINGER SOURDOUGH CAKE

MAKES 1 loaf
EQUIPMENT 2-pound loaf pan

We use a big mix of ground spices to create the depth and complexity this cake needs, and the cranberries add pockets of sweetness to tone down the gingery heat. The combination of the sweet starter and the date syrup brings a lovely, deep dark color, and the sourdough gives it a great texture.

Bake this in a loaf pan so you can slice it thick and slather it with butter. Once again, it's a cake that develops its flavor over time and keeps really well in an airtight container.

DAY 1

- ¼ cup (50 g) (packed) coconut sugar
- Scant ¼ cup (50 g) whole milk
- ⅓ cup (50 g) spelt flour
- Active Sweet Starter (page 184)

Add the sugar, milk, and flour to the whole quantity of the sweet starter. Mix well and leave loosely covered at room temperature overnight.

DAY 2

- 5½ ounces (150 g) recipe starter from Day 1
- 7 tablespoons (100 g) Greek yogurt
- ⅔ cup (200 g) date syrup
- 2 large (110 g) eggs
- ½ cup (100 g) coconut oil, melted
- 2 teaspoons (10 g) vanilla extract
- 1¾ cups (225 g) spelt flour
- 2 teaspoons (10 g) baking powder
- Pinch (0.25 g) of salt
- 1 tablespoon (15 g) ground ginger
- ½ teaspoon (2.5 g) ground turmeric
- 1 teaspoon (5 g) ground cinnamon
- 1 teaspoon (5 g) ground mixed spice (page 144)
- ½ teaspoon (2.5 g) ground cardamom
- 1¼ cups (150 g) dried cranberries

1. Preheat the oven to 400°F and line a 2-pound loaf pan with parchment paper.

2. In a large bowl, combine the recipe starter with the yogurt, date syrup, eggs, oil, and vanilla.

3. In another bowl, mix together the flour, baking powder, salt, spices, and cranberries. Add the dry ingredients to the starter mix and combine well.

4. Pour the mixture into the pan and bake for about 50 minutes until a skewer comes out clean. Cool in the pan for 10 to 15 minutes and turn out onto a wire rack.

NUTRITION NOTE

With so many ingredients from different food groups, this is a great contributor toward the target we believe we should all be aiming for of eating one hundred and fifty different ingredients a week.

APPLE SOURDOUGH CAKE

MAKES 1 × 8-inch round cake **EQUIPMENT** 8-inch round springform pan

≡

This is the ultimate apple cake, and Leo's favorite. The use of the sweet starter transports this cake to another level, giving it a rich, indulgent flavor without being too cloying sweet. The natural sourness of the sourdough enhances the floral flavors in the apple.

If you like a bit of crunch in your cakes, chop the apple chunks slightly thicker, if you prefer them softer, cut them thinner; we like a combination of the two. The flavor of this cake actually improves after a couple of days, but don't worry if you can't wait that long as it's also delicious still warm from the oven, especially with a dollop of fresh cream or coconut yogurt. As an added bonus, it also freezes well.

DAY 1

- ¼ cup (50 g) (packed) coconut sugar
- Scant ¼ cup (50 g) whole milk
- ⅓ cup (50 g) spelt flour
- Active Sweet Starter (page 184)

Add the sugar, milk, and flour to the whole quantity of the sweet starter. Mix well and leave loosely covered at room temperature overnight.

DAY 2

- 5½ ounces (150 g) recipe starter from Day 1
- Scant 2 cups (180 g) coconut oil, melted
- 2 large (110 g) eggs
- 2 teaspoons (10 g) vanilla extract
- 1 cup (200 g) (packed) coconut sugar, plus more for topping
- 1¾ cups (225 g) spelt flour
- 2 teaspoons (10 g) baking powder
- Pinch (0.25 g) of salt
- 2 teaspoons (10 g) ground cinnamon
- 1 apple, unpeeled, cored, and chopped into chunks
- 1 apple, unpeeled, cored, and sliced thinly, for decorating the top

1. Preheat the oven to 400°F and line an 8-inch round springform pan with parchment paper.
2. In a large bowl, combine the recipe starter, oil, eggs, vanilla, and sugar. Mix well.
3. In another bowl, stir together the flour, baking powder, salt, and cinnamon. Stir in the apple chunks—by coating them in flour you prevent them from sinking to the bottom of the cake as it bakes.
4. Add the flour and apple mix to the wet mix and combine well.
5. Pour the mixture into the pan, top with the apple slices, and sprinkle with more sugar.
6. Bake for 45 minutes until a skewer comes out clean. Let cool in the pan for 10 to 15 minutes, then turn out onto a wire rack.

CARROT AND WALNUT SOURDOUGH CAKE

☰

We readily admit that carrot cakes are up there as one of our favorite styles of cakes, so we are always looking for new twists on the classic. That's why making a sourdough carrot cake was high on our priority list. The sourdough heightens the cakey carrot flavors, which bring together the warm spices. This one's quite a dense cake. It will last you a while and subtly change flavor over a few days, becoming richer.

DAY 1

- Generous ⅓ cup (75 g) (packed) coconut sugar
- 5 tablespoons (75 g) whole milk
- ½ cup (75 g) spelt flour
- Active Sweet Starter (page 184)

Add the sugar, milk, and flour to the whole quantity of the sweet starter. Mix well and leave loosely covered at room temperature overnight.

NUTRITION NOTE

A lot of people have learned that root vegetables have a high GI and therefore assume they should steer away from them. This comes up a lot in discussions over the counter. In fact, although high-GI foods do raise blood sugar levels more, it's their glycemic load we should really be looking at. This takes into account the amount of carbohydrate they contain. Carrots may have a GI of 71, but their glycemic load is just 7.2, which is low. So it's fine to eat plenty! What's more, when they are subjected to fermentation (in this case the sourdough), their GI levels further reduce.

MAKES 1 loaf **EQUIPMENT** 2-pound loaf pan

DAY 2

- 8 ounces (225 g) recipe starter from Day 1
- Scant 2 cups (180 g) coconut oil, melted
- ¾ cup (150 g) (packed) coconut sugar
- 2 large (110 g) eggs
- 1½ cups (200 g) grated carrot
- 1¾ cups (230 g) spelt flour
- 1 teaspoon (5 g) ground cinnamon
- 1 teaspoon (5 g) mixed spice (page 144)
- 2 teaspoons (10 g) baking powder
- Pinch (0.25 g) of salt
- ½ cup (75 g) walnuts, chopped
- Yogurt Frosting (page 218)

1. Preheat the oven to 400°F and line a 2-pound loaf pan with parchment paper.
2. In a large bowl, mix together the recipe starter, oil, sugar, eggs, and carrot.
3. In another bowl, whisk together the flour, spices, baking powder, and salt, then stir in the walnuts.
4. Add the dry mix to the wet mix and combine thoroughly.
5. Pour the mixture into the pan and bake for 50 to 60 minutes until a skewer inserted into the middle comes out clean. Cool in the pan for 10 to 15 minutes, then turn out onto a wire rack. As soon as the cake is completely cool, top with the Yogurt Frosting.

SOURDOUGH PEANUT BUTTER BLONDIES

≡

There is a lot of confusion about what blondies actually are. Many recipes use white chocolate, but in fact blondies are brownies made with brown sugar and without any chocolate at all, hence their paler color. Coconut sugar works so well in them, as it has an intense, caramel flavor that is amplified by the sweet starter. Peanut butter adds a savory twist that stops the blondies becoming overly sweet, as well as a little protein boost.

A good peanut butter contains only peanuts and is very easy to make at home by blending peanuts (toasted if preferred) in a high-speed blender. If you're not making your own, use one with no added sugar or salt.

DAY 1

- Generous ⅓ cup (75 g) (packed) coconut sugar
- 5 tablespoons (75 g) whole milk
- ½ cup (75 g) spelt flour
- Active Sweet Starter (page 184)

Add the sugar, milk, and flour to the whole quantity of the sweet starter. Mix well and leave loosely covered at room temperature overnight.

DAY 2

- 8 ounces (225 g) recipe starter from Day 1
- Generous ¾ cup (190 g) peanut butter
- Generous ⅓ cup (75 g) coconut oil, melted
- 2 teaspoons (10 g) vanilla extract
- Scant 2 cups (180 g) (packed) coconut sugar
- ½ cup (70 g) spelt flour
- ½ teaspoon (2.5 g) baking powder
- Pinch (0.25 g) of salt
- Raw peanuts, for topping

1. Preheat the oven to 400°F. Line a 10½ × 8-inch brownie tray with parchment paper.

2. In a bowl, mix the recipe starter, peanut butter, oil, vanilla, and sugar.

3. In another bowl, mix together the flour, baking powder, and salt, then add to the wet mix and combine well. The mixture will be quite thick because of the peanut butter, but this is fine. Pour the mix into the pan and spread out evenly with a spatula or dough scraper. Top with the raw peanuts and bake for 20 minutes. The blondies should still be soft and gooey in the middle when they come out of the oven.

4. Let the blondies cool in the pan. Once cool, turn them out onto a cutting board and cut into squares.

NUTRITION NOTE

Peanut butter is something of a superfood. It has protein, fiber, vitamins, minerals, and healthy fats.

MAKES 8 blondies **EQUIPMENT** 10½ × 8-inch brownie tray

VANILLA AND RASPBERRY CHEESECAKE

MAKES 1 large cheesecake or 12 mini cheesecakes

EQUIPMENT 8½-inch tart pan with removable bottom or 12-cup silicone muffin mold, food processor, and high-speed blender

☰

This raw cheesecake is much lighter and fresher-tasting than a dairy cheesecake and the cashew topping is such a good medium for color and decoration. Even though it looks stunning as a whole cake, we sometimes make individual ones in a silicone muffin tray.

It makes a fantastic light dessert, or, with a bit of imaginative decoration it makes a tastefully subtle celebration cake too—with a bit of forward planning needed for the freezing time.

Like so many of our recipes, it is also easily adapted. We love the tartness of raspberry. Freeze-dried raspberry powder may seem like a futuristic ingredient, but it is well worth having in your pantry as it has so many uses. Try stirring it into oatmeal and adding to your smoothies.

FOR THE BASE

- 1¼ cups (150 g) unsalted cashews
- Generous 1 cup (150 g) pitted dates
- 2 tablespoons (25 g) coconut oil
- 1 tablespoon (15 g) maca powder

FOR THE FILLING

- Scant 2 cups (225 g) unsalted cashews, soaked for at least 4 hours but preferably overnight
- Juice of 1 lemon
- ½ cup (100 g) coconut oil, melted
- 1¾ cups (400 g) whole coconut milk
- ⅓ cup (100 g) maple syrup
- 1 teaspoon (5 g) vanilla extract
- 2 tablespoons (25 g) freeze-dried raspberry powder
- Fresh raspberries, for topping

1. Grease an 8½-inch tart pan or a 12-cup silicone muffin mold with a neutral oil such as sunflower oil. Do not use coconut oil as this will freeze solid and will not have a lubricating effect.

2. To make the base, blend the cashews in a food processor to the texture of coarse sand. Add the dates, oil, and maca and continue to blend until the mixture comes together as a smooth mass. Pour the mixture into the springform pan or divide evenly among the muffin cups and press down well. Place in the freezer as you make the filling.

3. To make the filling, drain the cashews and rinse under running water. Put them in a high-speed blender along with all the other filling ingredients, apart from the raspberry powder and fresh raspberries. Blitz well on high speed until completely smooth and creamy. Pour the mixture straight into the springform pan or muffin mold cups, to halfway up the side—you should have about half the cashew mix left. Return the mold to the freezer for 20 minutes. In the meantime, add the raspberry powder to the mixture left in the blender and blitz again, until the raspberry is spread evenly throughout.

4. After 20 minutes take the tray out of the freezer and pour the raspberry cashew mix on top of the set vanilla layer, right to the top of the pan or cups. Return the mold to the freezer for at least 4 hours, but preferably overnight.

5. Take the mold out of the freezer 20 minutes before you want to serve them, and top with the fresh raspberries.

VARIATIONS

PEANUT BUTTER CHEESECAKE

Add 2 tablespoons peanut butter, either to all the mix or just to the second half, as you prefer.

MATCHA GREEN TEA AND LEMON CHEESECAKE

Add 1 tablespoon matcha green tea powder and the zest of a lemon, either to all the mix or just to the second half, as you prefer.

RHUBARB AND GINGER CHEESECAKE (PICTURED RIGHT)

Add 1/4 cup (20 g) fresh grated ginger to the cashew mix, either to all the mix or just to the second half, as you prefer. Gently heat some rhubarb that has been cut into 2-inch pieces with 1 tablespoon maple syrup and 2 tablespoons water, until soft, then set aside to cool. When the cheesecake has set, top with the room-temperature rhubarb and serve.

NUTRITION NOTE

Too often we throw away the most nutritious part of a plant—the peel of an apple, the tops of scallions, the broccoli stem—but rhubarb is an exception. The leaves contain a mildly toxic acid that should be avoided.

RAW MILLIONAIRE'S SHORTBREAD

MAKES 15 pieces **EQUIPMENT** 10½ × 8-inch brownie tray and a food processor **GF DF V+**

We only make these incredibly indulgent treats on weekends and sometimes almost the whole tray is preordered. They are packed with nuts and dates and so deliciously rich that a small piece will satisfy all your sweet cravings. The maca we use in the base gives them a real cookie flavor and also helps balance out some of the sweetness from the dates.

FOR THE BASE

- 1½ cups (200 g) almonds
- 1¼ cups (175 g) pitted dates
- 7 tablespoons (100 g) almond butter
- 1 tablespoon (15 g) coconut oil
- 1 tablespoon (15 g) maca powder

FOR THE MIDDLE LAYER

- 1½ cups (200 g) pitted dates
- Scant 1 cup (200 g) almond butter
- 1 tablespoon (15 g) coconut oil

FOR THE TOP LAYER

- ½ cup (100 g) coconut oil, melted
- ⅔ cup (60 g) raw cacao powder
- 2 tablespoons (25 g) date syrup

1. Line a 10½ × 8-inch brownie tray with parchment paper.
2. For the base, put the nuts in the food processor and blitz until they are the consistency of coarse sand.
3. Add the dates, butter, oil, and maca and blitz again until the mixture is smooth and starting to come together. You may need to scrape the sides of the bowl down a few times. There should be no large chunks of dates.
4. Empty the mixture into the brownie tray and press down really well, so that it is completely compacted. Place in the freezer while you make the middle layer.
5. For the middle layer, place all the ingredients in the food processor with scant ¼ cup (50 g) water. Blitz until the mixture is smooth and completely combined.
6. Take the base out of the freezer and spread the mixture evenly over the top. You may need to dab off some of the excess liquid after you have done this to prevent it from forming an oily layer. Place the tray back in the freezer.
7. To make the top layer, melt all the ingredients together over gentle heat in a small pan, stirring occasionally. You do not want the mixture to boil; ideally it shouldn't go above 104°F or it won't be considered raw.
8. When the oil has melted and the mixture is well combined, pour it over the other layers and return the tray to the freezer for at least 1 hour.
9. When you are ready to serve, take the tray out of the freezer and turn the slab out onto a cutting board. Slice with a warm knife to prevent the chocolate from cracking.

NUTRITION NOTE

Almonds are the à la mode nut, and rightly so . . . they contain lots of healthy fats, fiber, protein, magnesium, and vitamin E. Healthy fats help to keep blood pressure and cholesterol levels low.

CHOCOLATE AND GINGER TART

≡

This is a vegan chocoholic's dream. It is rich and creamy, and yet there's no dairy in it. This is the favorite tart of the most cheerful customer we have at the bakery, so we'll often make it just to thank her for brightening our day when she comes in.

It can be made up to a week in advance, and kept in the refrigerator.

FOR THE BASE

- 1⅓ cups (175 g) almonds
- 1¼ cups (175 g) pitted dates
- 3½ tablespoons (50 g) almond butter
- 2 tablespoons (25 g) coconut oil

FOR THE CHOCOLATE FILLING

- 1½ cups (375 g) almond milk
- 2 tablespoons (25 g) cornstarch
- 1 teaspoon (5 g) vanilla extract
- ¾ ounce (20 g) fresh ginger, peeled and grated
- 1¾ cups (285 g) coconut sugar–sweetened chocolate chips or raw chocolate
- 2 tablespoons coconut oil

1. Grease and line the bottom of a 9½-inch tart pan.
2. To make the base, blitz the almonds in a food processor until they resemble coarse sand. Add the dates, butter, and oil and continue to blend until the mixture comes together as a smooth mass. Press it into the bottom of the prepared pan, smooth it over carefully, and put it in the freezer while you make the chocolate filling.
3. In a small pan, heat the milk with the cornstarch, vanilla, and fresh ginger. By adding the ginger here you infuse the milk with it, which spreads the flavor evenly through the filling. Bring the milk to a boil, whisking occasionally to prevent the cornstarch from forming clumps and burning on the bottom of the pan. As soon as the mixture comes to a boil and has slightly thickened, take it off the heat.
4. Put the chocolate chips in a heatproof bowl with the oil. Pour the boiling milk mixture over the chocolate and let stand for 2 minutes to melt the chocolate, then mix well into one homogenous mass.
5. Pour the filling over the tart base and let chill in the refrigerator overnight. Turn it out of the pan onto a plate just before you are ready to serve it.

NUTRITION NOTE

Ginger is thought to be one of the healthiest spices on the planet and experimental studies have shown that ginger inhibits the inflammation process.

MAKES 1 × 9½-inch round tart

EQUIPMENT 9½-inch round tart pan with removable bottom and a food processor **GF DF V+**

RAW CARROT CAKE

MAKES 1 × 8-inch round cake

EQUIPMENT 8-inch round springform pan and a food processor **GF DF V+**

≡

It never ceases to amaze us how knowledgeable many teenagers now are when it comes to healthy food. Martha, who was 17 when she joined our team, is a perfect example. She happens to be slightly obsessed with this raw carrot cake, and it was her choice for her 18th birthday cake.

It really stands out on the counter; with its bright green matcha topping and orange base, it's wonderfully kitsch! When sprinkled with dried edible rose and cornflower petals it is a beautiful, natural centerpiece.

- Scant 1 cup (120 g) walnuts
- 1 cup (120 g) pecans
- 20 pitted dates, soaked in hot water for 15 minutes, and well drained
- About 1⅔ cups (220 g) grated carrots
- 1 teaspoon (5 g) ground cinnamon
- ½ teaspoon (2.5 g) ground ginger
- 1 tablespoon (15 g) coconut oil, melted

FOR THE TOPPING

- ½ batch of Vanilla Cashew Nut Frosting (page 214)
- ½ tablespoon (7.5 g) matcha green tea powder

1. Line an 8-inch round springform pan with parchment paper.

2. In a food processor, process the walnuts and pecans until fine but not sticky. Then add the dates and process again. Empty the contents from the food processor and add to the rest of the ingredients and mix by hand. You might need to scrape the sides of the bowl down a few times. Empty the mixture into the pan and smooth the top.

3. For the frosting, blend the Vanilla Cashew Nut Frosting with the matcha powder until mixed. Pour directly on top of the carrot mix and smooth the top. Place in the refrigerator for at least an hour, or until you are ready to serve. Turn out of the pan just before serving.

NUTRITION NOTE

The body of the cake is carrots, walnuts, and pecans (plenty of fiber) so it's a very different kind of cake from one made with flour. It's moist and gooey, and we defy anyone not to devour an oversized slice as soon as it's made.

RAW BEET, STRAWBERRY, AND COCONUT CAKE WITH COCONUT CASHEW NUT FROSTING

≡

An ingredient like beet, with such a strong color, is great for adding color to cakes—choose the purple variety. With such a vibrant red base and clean white topping, it's a real showstopper. We sometimes decorate it with fresh strawberries and edible rose petals, for an extra color burst.

- 1½ cups (200 g) pitted dates
- 1 ounce (25 g) freeze-dried strawberry powder
- 2 tablespoons (25 g) coconut oil
- 2 cups (150 g) dry unsweetened coconut
- 1 cup (100 g) almond meal
- 1½ cups (230 g) grated raw beet

FOR THE TOPPING

- ½ batch of Vanilla Cashew Nut Frosting (page 214)
- ⅔ cup (50 g) dry unsweetened coconut
- Dry unsweetened coconut or fresh strawberries, for decoration (optional)

1. Line an 8-inch round springform pan with parchment paper. We find springform pans are best when making raw cakes as it's easier to get the cake out.

2. In a food processor, process together the dates, strawberry powder, oil, dry unsweetened coconut, and almond meal until they form a smooth paste. Add the grated beet to the mix and pulse until it is well combined but has not lost its grated form. This is because you want some of the texture from the grated beet in the finished cake.

3. Empty the cake batter into the pan and smooth the top well. Place in the refrigerator.

NUTRITION NOTE

Deeply colored fruit and vegetables are high in antioxidants, making them an important part of our diet. We should all be aiming to eat something from every color of the rainbow, every day.

MAKES 1 × 8-inch round cake

EQUIPMENT 8-inch round springform pan and a food processor **GF DF V+**

RAW BEET, STRAWBERRY, AND COCONUT CAKE WITH COCONUT CASHEW NUT FROSTING

4 To make the frosting, take half a batch of Cashew Nut Frosting and stir in the dry unsweetened coconut. Don't use the blender here as you want the coconut to give texture to the frosting. Pour the frosting over the top of the cake and level it. Let chill in the refrigerator for at least 4 hours, or overnight.

5 You can make this cake in advance and keep it in the refrigerator for 4 to 5 days, or in the freezer for 4 weeks. Defrost for 1 to 2 hours in the refrigerator before eating.

6 When you are ready to serve, turn out the cake and decorate it with more dry unsweetened coconut or some fresh strawberries.

RAW BANOFFEE PIE

MAKES 1 × 8-inch round cake

EQUIPMENT 8-inch round tart pan with a removable bottom, a food processor, and high-speed blender

GF DF V+

≡

When we were talking to our team about which recipes they wanted us to include in this book, this one was high on everyone's list. We cater to a lot of food allergies and intolerances in the bakery and many of our customers thought they would never be eating something like banoffee pie again. This pie looks simple from the outside, but it's spectacularly delicious when you slice into it—and it's very bananery!

FOR THE BASE

- 1½ cups (200 g) almonds
- 1½ cups (200 g) pitted dates
- 3½ tablespoons (50 g) almond butter
- 3 tablespoons (45 g) coconut oil
- 1 tablespoon (15 g) maca powder

FOR THE BANANA CARAMEL

- ¾ cup (100 g) pitted dates
- 7 tablespoons (100 g) almond butter
- 1 banana
- ½ tablespoon (7.5 g) coconut oil
- 2 extra bananas, sliced, for layering

FOR THE BANANA CREAM

- 1½ cups (175 g) unsalted cashews, soaked for at least 4 hours but preferably overnight
- Juice of 1 lemon
- ⅓ cup (75 g) coconut oil, melted
- 1¼ cups (300 g) whole coconut milk
- ⅓ cup (100 g) maple syrup
- 1 banana

1. Grease and line the bottom of an 8-inch round tart pan with a removable bottom.
2. To make the base, blend the almonds in a food processor until they are the texture of coarse sand. Add the rest of the base ingredients and continue to process until they come together as one smooth mass.
3. Scrape the mixture with a spatula into the pan and press so that the mixture covers the bottom and the sides of the pan. Make sure it is compacted well. Put in the freezer while you make the caramel.
4. Put all the banana caramel ingredients, except the sliced bananas, in a food processor with 2 tablespoons (25 g) water and blend until smooth and homogenous. Take the base out of the freezer and smooth the caramel mixture into the base. Top with the two sliced bananas and return to the freezer.
5. To make the banana cream, put all the ingredients in a high-speed blender and process until smooth and creamy. Pour over the top of the caramel and bananas. Return to the freezer for at least 4 hours, preferably overnight.
6. Remove from the freezer 1 hour before serving and carefully remove from the pan.

NUTRITION NOTE

The potassium found in bananas is essential in keeping blood pressure in check and maintaining a good heart function.

RAW PEANUT BUTTER AND CHOCOLATE CUPS

MAKES 12 standard cups or 24 mini cups

EQUIPMENT 2 × 12-cup mini muffin or 1 × 12-cup standard muffin pan and a food processor

GF DF V+

☰

The heavenly combination of peanut butter and chocolate is always decadent, and the unprocessed versions of both ingredients are wonderfully nutritious. A peanut butter and cacao smoothie has been known to get us through a long shift. This is our take on the peanut butter cup.

We usually make them in a mini muffin pan, but a standard muffin pan will work too. They make fab individual desserts.

When we can, we make our own date syrup. Simply blitz some soaked pitted dates in a high-speed blender with a little water.

FOR THE PEANUT BUTTER BASE

- Scant 1 cup (200 g) peanut butter
- 1⅓ cups (180 g) pitted dates
- 1 cup (100 g) oats
- 1 cup (100 g) almond meal
- 1 teaspoon (5 g) vanilla extract
- 2 tablespoons (25 g) coconut oil

FOR THE CHOCOLATE TOPPING

- ½ cup (100 g) coconut oil
- ⅓ cup (30 g) raw cacao powder
- 2 tablespoons (25 g) date syrup

1. Grease a mini muffin or standard muffin tray with a neutral-flavored oil such as sunflower oil (not coconut oil as this will go solid and won't prevent the mixture sticking).

2. In a food processor, blend together all the peanut butter base ingredients until they come together in a smooth mass with no lumps of date.

3. Divide the mixture evenly among the cups in the tray and press down firmly. Place the tray in the freezer while you make the chocolate topping.

4. For the topping, place all the ingredients in a small pan and warm over gentle heat until the oil is completely melted. The date syrup can sink to the bottom, so make sure you mix them together really well.

5. Pour the chocolate over the peanut butter mix and return the tray to the freezer for at least 1 hour.

6. These lovely cups keep really well in the freezer for up to a month, or in the refrigerator for up to 2 weeks. Defrost for 1 to 2 hours in the refrigerator before eating.

NUTRITION NOTE

Dates are rich in minerals, vitamins, and fiber. The humble peanut is often eclipsed these days by the more fashionable nuts, but it can punch its nutritional weight alongside all of them!

VANILLA CASHEW NUT FROSTING

EQUIPMENT high-speed blender

GF DF V+

≡

We have to get really creative when it comes to "icing" our cakes as we don't use confectioners' sugar. This recipe is one of our go-to frosting recipes; it's really easy to make and absolutely delicious. The basic recipe is for a vanilla frosting, but it can easily be adapted to different flavors—we particularly like to add matcha for a vibrant green color!

- 1¼ cups (150 g) unsalted cashews, soaked for at least 4 hours but preferably overnight
- 1¼ cups (300 g) whole coconut milk
- 2 tablespoons (25 g) lemon juice
- ¼ cup (75 g) maple syrup
- 1 teaspoon (5 g) vanilla extract
- ½ cup (100 g) coconut oil, melted

Drain and rinse the soaked cashews. Put them in a blender with all the other ingredients and blend until completely smooth and creamy. Pour into a container and chill in the refrigerator until firm. We usually leave the frosting in the refrigerator overnight, but around 4 hours should do the trick.

OPTIONAL FLAVORINGS

3 tablespoons raw cacao powder (for Chocolate Cashew Nut Frosting)

1 tablespoon freeze-dried raspberry powder (for Raspberry Cashew Nut Frosting)

1 tablespoon matcha green tea powder (for Matcha Cashew Nut Frosting)

CHOCOLATE AND AVOCADO GANACHE

EQUIPMENT high-speed blender

GF DF

≡

This recipe was developed to frost the chocolate avocado cake, but it went down so well with customers and team that we now use it on all of our chocolate cakes. And if you ever need a quick dessert, you can whip this up in 5 minutes and serve it topped with raspberries.

The avocado gives a richness usually provided by cream.

- 2 ripe medium Hass avocados, peeled and pitted
- 3½ ounces (100 g) chocolate, melted
- Scant ¼ cup (50 g) maple syrup
- 2 tablespoons (25 g) coconut oil, melted

Put all the ingredients in a high-speed blender or food processor and blitz until smooth. You can either use it straightaway or leave it overnight in the refrigerator.

MAPLE CREAM CHEESE FROSTING

≡

This is our take on classic cream cheese frosting. It's a lot less sweet and totally delicious.

GF

- 2 tablespoons (25 g) maple syrup
- 1 cup (225 g) organic whole cream cheese, straight from the refrigerator
- 2 tablespoons (25 g) coconut oil, melted

1. Stir the maple syrup into the chilled cream cheese until completely combined.
2. Add the melted oil and mix very quickly to prevent lumps from forming.

COFFEE CREAM CHEESE FROSTING

≡

This is a double portion of frosting for sandwiching and topping the Coffee and Pecan Nut Cake (page 142).

- ¼ cup (60 g) maple syrup
- 2 cups (450 g) organic whole cream cheese, straight from the refrigerator
- ¼ cup (60 g) coconut oil, melted
- ¼ cup (60 g) espresso, brewed and cooled (or cafetière coffee)

1. Stir the maple syrup into the chilled cream cheese until completely combined.
2. Add the melted oil and mix very quickly to prevent lumps from forming.
3. Add the cold coffee and mix thoroughly.

YOGURT FROSTING

≡

This is very similar to our cream cheese frosting, but it has a much lighter and fresher flavor that works really well with sourdough cakes. You want a fairly thick yogurt; we like to use either Greek yogurt or coconut yogurt.

GF

- 1 cup (225 g) yogurt, straight from the refrigerator
- 2 tablespoons (25 g) maple syrup or honey
- 1 teaspoon (5 g) vanilla extract
- 3 tablespoons (45 g) coconut oil, melted

1. Mix together the yogurt, maple syrup or honey, and vanilla until they are thoroughly combined.

2. Add the melted oil and mix together quickly. As you are mixing, the yogurt should become much thicker.

CHOCOLATE CREAM CHEESE FROSTING

≡

This simple but heavenly chocolate frosting is a variation of our Maple Cream Cheese Frosting (page 216).

GF

- 2 tablespoons (25 g) maple syrup
- 2 tablespoons (25 g) raw cacao powder
- 1 cup (225 g) organic whole cream cheese, straight from the refrigerator
- 2 tablespoons (25 g) coconut oil, melted

1. Stir the maple syrup and cacao powder into the chilled cream cheese until completely combined.

2. Add the melted oil and mix very quickly to prevent lumps from forming.

LEMON CREAM CHEESE FROSTING

≡

This zingy, citrus version of our cream cheese frosting is perfect for our Lemon Sourdough Cake (page 188) among others.

GF

- 2 tablespoons (25 g) honey
- Zest of 1 lemon, finely grated
- 1 cup (225 g) organic whole cream cheese, straight from the refrigerator
- 2 tablespoons (25 g) coconut oil, melted

1. Stir the honey and lemon zest into the chilled cream cheese until completely combined.
2. Add the melted oil and mix very quickly to prevent lumps from forming.

RASPBERRY CHIA JAM

≡

This 5-minute jam is so easy to make and incredibly versatile. As well as making a delicious filling for our Victoria sponge, it's also great for spreading on toast or even as a topping for ice cream.

We most often make it with raspberries, but you can use any fruit that's in season. Blueberries with a teaspoon of ground cinnamon is a delicious variation, or plums with a grating of fresh ginger. You can use either fresh or frozen fruit. The chia seeds are what give this the consistency of jam.

- 1⅔ cups (200 g) raspberries
- 1 tablespoon (15 g) maple syrup
- 2 tablespoons (25 g) chia seeds

1. In a small saucepan, warm the raspberries with the maple syrup over medium heat until they are very soft and releasing their juices.
2. Mash the fruit lightly and add the chia seeds. Turn the heat down and cook the jam for another 5 minutes. That's it.
3. Once the jam is cool you can use it straightaway or store it in the refrigerator for up to a week or two.

Sourdough cinnamon bun
£2.20

KALE AND FETA SCONES

MAKES about 8 scones

EQUIPMENT baking sheet and a round cutter

On the front counter at the bakery we mainly focus on sweet treats, but we appreciate that there are times when you just want something savory and easy to eat. We developed these scones to fill that need. They are filling on their own as a snack, but also make a great accompaniment to soup. They are really simple to make; in fact they're perfect for making with children as a stepping-stone from sweet baking to making bread. We like to bake these a little oversized.

- 3 cups (390 g) spelt flour
- 2½ teaspoons (12.5 g) baking powder
- ½ teaspoon (2.5 g) salt
- 1 cup (230 g) organic whole cream cheese
- ½ cup (115 g) cold butter
- 1⅓ cups (200 g) crumbled feta cheese
- 1¾ ounces (50 g) kale, shredded (you could replace this with spinach if you prefer)
- 1 large (55 g) egg
- ¼ cup (60 g) whole milk

1. Preheat the oven to 450°F. Line a baking sheet with parchment paper.

2. In a bowl, combine the flour, baking powder, and salt. Rub in the cream cheese and butter with your fingers, then stir in the crumbled feta cheese, holding some back for later, and the kale.

3. Add the egg and milk and knead the dough until just combined. It's important not to knead the dough too much or the scones will be heavy.

4. Pat out the dough onto a floured counter until 1 inch thick. Use a cutter to cut out circles, but be sure not to twist the cutter as you do so as this will constrain the gluten and prevent the scones from rising as well. Top with the reserved cheese, place on the sheet, and bake for 16 to 18 minutes until golden brown. Transfer them to a wire rack as soon as they come out of the oven.

NUTRITION NOTE

The kale gives these a great nutritional boost. It is great for aiding digestion and high in fiber as well as being packed with a wide variety of beneficial vitamins and minerals.

SPINACH, YOGURT, AND GOAT CHEESE LOAF CAKE

MAKES 1 loaf

EQUIPMENT 2-pound loaf pan

≡

After being advised to minimize dairy for a while, I developed a love for goat cheese because it's generally a less farmed and less processed form of dairy. It became my default when eating out, and has remained a firm favorite ever since. You could use feta in this, or any cheese.

You can vary the leaves, perhaps use kale or chard, as well as the cheese and the herbs. Just tailor to what you like best. It is really delicious on its own as a snack, but equally as tasty with some smashed avocado.

- Scant 2 cups (250 g) spelt flour
- 2 teaspoons (10 g) baking powder
- Pinch (0.25 g) of salt
- Pinch (0.25 g) of ground black pepper
- 3½ ounces (100 g) spinach, chopped
- Scant ½ cup (10 g) fresh basil, chopped
- Scant ½ cup (10 g) fresh parsley, chopped
- Scant ½ cup (10 g) fresh dill, chopped
- 1 cup (150 g) crumbly goat cheese, crumbled
- Generous 1 cup (250 g) Greek yogurt
- ½ cup (120 g) extra virgin olive oil
- 2 large (110 g) eggs

1. Preheat the oven to 425°F and line a 2-pound loaf pan with parchment paper.
2. In a large bowl, mix together the flour, baking powder, salt, and pepper. Add the spinach, herbs, and two-thirds of the goat cheese and stir through.
3. In another bowl, beat together the yogurt, olive oil, and eggs. Add this mix to the flour and spinach mix and combine well. The mix will be quite dry.
4. Press the batter into the prepared pan—it is quite nice to give it a rough top for some crunch—and top with the remainder of the cheese.
5. Bake for 50 minutes, or until a skewer inserted into the middle comes out clean. Cool in the pan for 10 to 15 minutes and then turn out onto a wire rack to cool.

NUTRITION NOTE

Spinach is loaded with good things for every part of your body. It's abundant in antioxidants to protect your body from free radicals, the folate in it is good for cardio, and magnesium helps to lower high blood pressure.

ROSEMARY, PARSNIP, AND PARMESAN LOAF CAKE

≡

This is the classic cheese, vegetable, and herb combination. This loaf cake goes particularly well with soup, though it's also delicious on its own, spread with butter.

We add "loaf" to the name because of its shape, but it's very much a savory cake. Unlike a real loaf, its raising agent is baking powder. You could also make smaller individual bakes in muffin pans (in which case reduce the bake time to 25 minutes).

- Scant 2 cups (250 g) spelt flour
- 2 teaspoons (10 g) baking powder
- 2½ ounces (75 g) Parmesan, freshly grated
- 1 tablespoon (15 g) fresh rosemary, minced
- Pinch (0.25 g) of salt
- Pinch (0.25 g) of ground black pepper
- 6 ounces (175 g) parsnips, grated
- 1 small white onion, minced
- 3 large (165 g) eggs
- 7 tablespoons (100 g) extra virgin olive oil

1. Preheat the oven to 400°F and line a 2-pound loaf pan with parchment paper.
2. In a large bowl, mix together the flour, baking powder, two-thirds of the Parmesan, the rosemary, salt, and pepper.
3. In another bowl, beat together the parsnips, onion, eggs, and olive oil.
4. Add the wet ingredients to the dry ingredients and mix well. Pour the batter into the pan, smooth over, and top with the rest of the Parmesan.
5. Bake for 50 minutes, or until a skewer inserted into the middle comes out clean. Cool in the pan for 10 to 15 minutes, then turn out onto a wire rack.
6. Serve warm with butter.

NUTRITION NOTE

Rosemary is one of the most recorded herbs from ancient times, and its benefits go way beyond just flavoring. It is long believed to have antioxidant and anti-inflammatory properties, so it is worth using even in small amounts. Rosemary is so abundantly grown that most people with mature plants are only too happy to give it away.

MAKES 1 loaf **EQUIPMENT** 2-pound loaf pan

CARROT, CUMIN, AND GOUDA LOAF CAKE

MAKES 1 loaf **EQUIPMENT** 2-pound loaf pan

This is a great bake for warming up on a wintery day, equally lovely with just a bit of butter or partnered with a thick, hearty soup.

It's a variation of another classic cheese, vegetable, and herb combination, our Rosemary, Parsnip, and Parmesan Loaf Cake (page 224). Carrot and cumin is a well-tried combination, but so too is the pairing of cumin and Gouda, which like so many fashionable combinations is in fact as ancient as it is modern.

- Scant 2 cups (250 g) spelt flour
- 2 teaspoons (10 g) baking powder
- 2½ ounces (75 g) young Gouda, freshly grated
- 2 teaspoons (10 g) cumin seeds
- Pinch (0.25 g) of salt
- Pinch (0.25 g) of ground black pepper
- 6 ounces (175 g) carrots, grated
- 1 small white onion, minced
- 3 large (165 g) eggs
- 7 tablespoons (100 g) extra virgin olive oil

1. Preheat the oven to 400°F and line a 2-pound loaf pan with parchment paper.
2. In a large bowl, mix together the flour, baking powder, two-thirds of the Gouda, the cumin, salt, and pepper.
3. In another bowl, beat together the carrots, onion, eggs, and olive oil.
4. Add the wet ingredients to the dry ingredients and mix well. Pour the batter into the pan, smooth over, and top with the rest of the Gouda.
5. Bake for 50 minutes, or until a skewer inserted into the middle comes out clean. Cool in the pan for 10 to 15 minutes, then turn out onto a wire rack.
6. Serve warm with butter.

NUTRITION NOTE

The carrot provides vitamin A while research shows that the oils in black cumin seeds have antibacterial and antiviral properties that can help fight infections.

Cookies, Bars & Bites

Cookies can be healthier, nutritious, and yet still taste terrific. Just as well, as there are times when only a cookie will do. What else would you dunk in a cup of tea or coffee on a rainy afternoon?

They are also the easiest way into healthy baking. We bake all these recipes using unrefined and unprocessed ingredients with high nutritional values—the flour, the sweetness, oils, fats, everything.

Our healthy cookies sell all day long, and inventing new flavors and combinations has become second nature. We used to discuss new ideas for hours, but once we'd established the principles of nutritional and tasty combinations, these decisions soon became intuitive.

With a tiny bit of imagination, you'll find yourself playing around with different textures, crumb sizes, and bite, and in no time you'll have opened up a whole new world of crunchy exhilaration. Bigger ones look great on a plate: smaller ones have more crunch. You'll find that quality, unrefined ingredients actually fill you up and keep you going for longer, too.

Two of the doughs will keep for up to 5 days in the refrigerator. All the other recipes are an instant mix and then straight to bake—less than 30 minutes and absolutely perfect for children. All keep well for 3 to 5 days in an airtight container.

SALTY SWEET SEAWEED COOKIES

MAKES 30 small cookies **EQUIPMENT** cookie cutters, baking sheet

These small, crispy cookies are really popular with customers looking for a salty-sweet hit, and they're always a conversation point. This was the first recipe using seaweed we ever created in the bakery, and now it's become one of our all-time favorite ingredients. Seaweed comes in many forms, but for this recipe we prefer to use Shony, which is a flake. The hint of umami in the seaweed combines really well with the fruity richness of the olive oil, and the sweetness comes from the intense caramel hit that baked coconut sugar uniquely delivers. Using spelt flour gives a nutty taste, and the mix of olive oil and butter is great for the texture and color.

NUTRITION NOTE

We believe that seaweed is about as nutrient-dense as it gets: it's a great source of iodine, an often overlooked mineral that many of us are deficient in, as well as magnesium and iron. It has more calcium than broccoli and it is packed with protein. Buy good-quality seeweed and eat in moderation.

- ¾ cup (1½ sticks/170 g) unsalted butter, at room temperature
- 1 cup (packed) (200 g) coconut sugar
- 2 tablespoons (20 g) seaweed flakes
- 1 tablespoon (15 g) salt
- 2 egg yolks
- 3 tablespoons (45 g) extra virgin olive oil
- Scant 2¼ cups (280 g) spelt flour

1. Beat together the butter, sugar, seaweed, and salt by hand or using electric beaters until light and fluffy. Add the egg yolks and olive oil and beat them in. Finally, add the flour and beat until it all combines into a dough.

2. Flatten the dough into a disk, wrap it in plastic wrap, and chill it in the refrigerator for at least an hour. This allows the gluten to relax, which makes the dough easier to handle and stops the cookies shrinking when they are baked. This dough will keep for up to 5 days in the refrigerator.

3. Preheat the oven to 400°F. Line a baking sheet with parchment paper.

4. Remove the dough from the refrigerator and roll it out to about 1/8 inch. Cut out the cookie shapes and place them on the baking sheet.

5. Bake for 12 to 14 minutes until golden brown.

6. Let the cookies cool and firm up on the sheet for 5 to 10 minutes, then transfer them to a wire rack.

TIGERNUT COOKIES

MAKES 12 to 15 cookies

EQUIPMENT baking sheet and 2-inch round cutters

GF DF V+

≡

These are our cookie of choice for having with a cup of tea. They are perfect for dunking, and won't dissolve into a soggy mess.

Tigernut flour naturally suits a range of intolerances, which explains its immediate impact on the healthy baking scene.

- ⅓ cup (75 g) almond butter
- 2 teaspoons (10 g) vanilla extract
- 3 tablespoons (45 g) almond milk
- 2 tablespoons (25 g) maple syrup
- Generous 1 cup (150 g) tigernut flour
- ½ cup (50 g) almond meal
- ⅔ cup (50 g) dry unsweetened coconut
- 1 teaspoon (5 g) baking powder
- Pinch (0.25 g) of salt

1. Preheat the oven to 400°F and line a baking sheet with parchment paper.
2. In a bowl, mix together the butter with the vanilla, milk, and maple syrup.
3. In another bowl, combine all the dry ingredients.
4. Add the dry ingredients to the wet ingredients and mix well with your hands until the mixture comes together in a stiff dough.
5. Roll the dough out on a floured counter to the thickness of ⅛ inch. Cut out 2-inch circles and place on the baking sheet.
6. Bake for 10 to 12 minutes until golden. Be careful as these can burn very quickly toward the end. Let cool on the baking sheet for about 10 minutes, then transfer to a wire rack. Store in an airtight container for up to a week.

NUTRITION NOTE

Tigernuts are not actually nuts but tubers, grown in a similar way to potatoes. They are rich in vitamin E and omega-9 fatty acids, as well as being high in fiber, and they are a natural prebiotic.

TAHINI AND OLIVE OIL COOKIES WITH SESAME SEEDS

MAKES 9 large cookies
EQUIPMENT baking sheet
GF DF V+

The idea for this recipe came from Martha, one of our front of house staff. Everyone at Modern Baker is passionate about healthy eating and our endless discussions, often with customers, are frequently a spark to creativity.

Tahini (sesame seed paste) and olive oil are familiar in hummus, but when taken down a different, sweeter path they come alive with a flavor that's distinctly delicious.

Maple syrup has one of the most complex flavors of all the natural sweeteners used in baking, and the touch of vanilla extract in this recipe makes all the difference.

- ½ cup (120 g) tahini (sesame seed paste)
- 1½ tablespoons (22.5 g) extra virgin olive oil
- Scant ½ cup (125 g) maple syrup
- 1 teaspoon (5 g) vanilla extract
- Generous 2 cups (215 g) almond meal
- 1 teaspoon (5 g) baking powder
- sesame seeds, for topping

1. Preheat the oven to 400°F. Line a baking sheet with parchment paper.
2. Melt the tahini in a pan with the olive oil, maple syrup, and vanilla, stirring occasionally. While you wait for that to come together, combine the almond meal and baking powder in another bowl.
3. Add the melted tahini mix to the dry ingredients and mix well.
4. Divide and shape the mixture into tablespoon-size balls and flatten each one in the damp palm of your hand to ½ inch thick. Dip one side of each cookie in a bowl of sesame seeds before placing them, seed side up, on the baking sheet.
5. Bake for 12 to 15 minutes until golden brown around the edges.
6. Let the cookies cool and firm up on the baking sheet for 5 to 10 minutes, then transfer them to a wire rack.

NUTRITION NOTE

Tahini is easy to make by whizzing toasted sesame seeds in a processor with a small amount of light oil. The intensely nutty paste that results is really rich in thiamin, zinc, and copper and important minerals such as calcium, as well as magnesium and iron.

GOLDEN TURMERIC AND HONEY COOKIES

≡

What better way to get health-giving turmeric into your diet than to make it part of a delicious sweet treat? And there isn't a spice with a more dramatic color. When we launched our hot turmeric mylk drink it wasn't long before customers started ordering them together, and dunking the cookies for a double turmeric hit.

- 2½ cups (250 g) almond meal
- 1 teaspoon (5 g) ground turmeric
- 1 teaspoon (5 g) ground cinnamon
- 1 teaspoon (5 g) ground black pepper
- ½ teaspoon (2.5 g) baking soda
- Pinch (0.25 g) of salt
- ⅓ cup (80 g) extra virgin olive oil
- ⅓ cup (100 g) runny organic honey

1. Preheat the oven to 400°F. Line a baking sheet with parchment paper.

2. Combine all the dry ingredients in a bowl and mix well. Add the olive oil and honey and stir until well mixed.

3. Divide and shape the mix into tablespoon-size balls and place them on the baking sheet. Flatten each ball with the damp palm of your hand to about ½ inch thick.

4. Bake for 12 to 13 minutes until golden around the edges.

5. Let the cookies cool and firm up on the baking sheet for 5 to 10 minutes, then transfer them to a wire rack.

NUTRITION NOTE

Research shows that turmeric, part of the ginger family, has many good health benefits. It's mainly the curcumin in turmeric that's responsible for this, and combining it with black pepper is thought to make it easier for the body to absorb.

MAKES 9 large cookies **EQUIPMENT** baking sheet **GF DF**

GINGER AND PEPPER SPICY COOKIES

MAKES 9 large cookies
EQUIPMENT baking sheet
GF DF V+

≡

These aren't the small hard ginger nuts that we all grew up with. They are larger and softer, with wonderful spices, as well as a real depth of flavor.

Although they're perfect on a cold wintry day with a mug of tea, we make them all year round. They are especially popular with our gluten-intolerant customers.

Most ginger cookies are sweetened with light corn syrup; for ours we like the earthy sweetness of date syrup. It works particularly well with the spices and almond meal.

- 2½ cups (250 g) almond meal
- 1 tablespoon (15 g) ground ginger
- 1 teaspoon (5 g) ground cinnamon
- ½ teaspoon (2.5 g) ground black pepper
- 1 teaspoon (5 g) mixed spice (page 144)
- ½ teaspoon (2.5 g) ground turmeric
- ½ teaspoon (2.5 g) baking soda
- Pinch (0.25 g) of salt
- ½ cup (90 g) coconut oil, melted
- ⅓ cup (100 g) date syrup

1. Preheat the oven to 400°F. Line a baking sheet with parchment paper.

2. Combine all the dry ingredients in a bowl. Add the melted oil and date syrup and stir them in well.

3. Divide and shape the mixture into tablespoon-size balls and place on the baking sheet. Flatten each ball with the damp palm of your hand so they are around ½ inch thick.

4. Bake for 12 to 13 minutes, until the color deepens.

5. Let the cookies cool and firm up on the sheet for 10 to 15 minutes, as they are particularly delicate when they come out of the oven, then transfer them to a wire rack.

GOLDEN LUCUMA AND CHIA COOKIES

MAKES 12 large cookies or pretzels

EQUIPMENT baking sheet and cookie cutters

Lindsay created this recipe when a friend brought her some lucuma powder following a trip to Peru, where it's known as "the gold of the Incas." It's used there as a sweetener in all sorts of cuisine and famed for its nutritional qualities.

It didn't take Lindsay long to see its remarkable qualities as a baking ingredient, not least as another natural substitute for refined sugar. It has quite a mellow, caramel taste with a hint of tangy fruitiness.

This is so far our only recipe where lucuma is the lead flavor, but we believe it has great potential. We already add it to our smoothies to make them creamier and healthier, so watch this space.

NUTRITION NOTE

Lucuma is very high in fiber. It also contains calcium and phosphorus needed for good functioning digestive enzymes and promotes healthy bones and teeth.

- 7 tablespoons (100 g) unsalted butter, at room temperature
- Generous ⅓ cup (packed) (75 g) coconut sugar
- 1 large (55 g) egg
- 1 teaspoon (5 g) vanilla extract
- ¼ cup (60 g) lucuma powder
- 1½ cups (200 g) spelt flour
- Chia seeds, for topping

1. Preheat the oven to 400°F. Line a baking sheet with parchment paper.
2. Beat the butter and sugar together by hand or using electric beaters until light and fluffy. Add the egg and vanilla and beat again until combined. Don't worry if the mixture splits slightly at this stage. Add the lucuma, then the flour, and beat again until all the ingredients are well combined.
3. Flatten the dough into a disk, wrap it in plastic wrap, and chill in the refrigerator for at least 1 hour.
4. For these cookies you have a couple of options for shaping. The first is to roll out the dough to about ⅛ inch, cut out cookies, and sprinkle them with chia seeds. The second is to divide the dough into 12 equal portions, roll each one into a sausage, and twist it into a bow shape by bringing one end over the middle, then bringing the other end over so that it overlaps it. Dip the top of each pretzel in the chia seeds.
5. Place, seed side up, on the sheet and bake for 12 to 15 minutes until they start to turn golden. The pretzel shapes may need slightly longer.
6. Let the cookies cool on the sheet for 5 to 10 minutes, then transfer them to a wire rack.

BRIGHT GREEN MATCHA COOKIES

MAKES 9 large cookies
EQUIPMENT baking sheet
GF DF

≡

The health world has gone matcha crazy recently. Modern Baker was Oxford's first matcha proponent with our matcha latte, a vivid green alternative to coffee, made with almond milk, a showstopper that soon caught on in a big way.

As a healthy bakery we have to work harder than a refined sugar–based bakery to bring color to our counter, but matcha is a gift, especially in the form of these large, bright green cookies. Most people think they're pistachio, and are intrigued by the notion of green tea flavoring a cookie! One taste and matcha becomes as much of a passion with them as it is with us.

They're great for children as well, colorful and healthy and not a single artificial color in sight, and easy enough for them to make too.

⇠ Pictured on previous spread

- Generous 2 cups (215 g) almond meal
- Scant 1 cup (75 g) slivered almonds
- 1 tablespoon (15 g) matcha green tea powder
- Generous ⅓ cup (packed) (75 g) coconut sugar
- 1 teaspoon (5 g) baking powder
- 1 large (55 g) egg
- ¼ cup (50 g) coconut oil, melted
- 1 teaspoon (5 g) vanilla extract
- 2 tablespoons (25 g) almond milk
- Blanched almonds, for topping

1. Preheat the oven to 400°F. Line a baking sheet with parchment paper.
2. Combine the almond meal, slivered almonds, matcha powder, sugar, and baking powder in a medium bowl and mix thoroughly.
3. In another bowl, whisk together the egg, melted oil, vanilla, and milk. Add the wet ingredients to the dry ingredients and mix well.
4. Divide and shape the mixture into tablespoon-size balls and place them on the baking sheet. Flatten each ball with your damp palm to about ½ inch thick and top each cookie with a blanched almond.
5. Bake for 12 to 13 minutes until darker around the edges.
6. Let the cookies cool and firm up on the baking sheet for 5 to 10 minutes, then transfer them to a wire rack.

NUTRITION NOTE

Matcha is made from chlorophyll-rich tea leaves, which are handpicked, steamed, dried, and ground into a fine green powder. There is no end to its claimed health benefits—immune boosting, mental clarity, and detoxification.

CINNAMON COOKIES WITH PECAN HALVES

MAKES 9 large cookies
EQUIPMENT baking sheet
GF DF V+

≡

These beauties are our most popular cookies in the bakery. Customers buy them in bulk and often ask to reserve some when they know we're baking them. They really capture what simple, deliciously healthy baking is all about—and all with less than half an hour to eating! On a busy day when we can suddenly find the counter empty, any of our staff can rustle up a batch of these in no time.

Pictured on previous spread

- 2½ cups (250 g) almond meal
- 1½ tablespoons (22.5 g) ground cinnamon
- 1 teaspoon (5 g) mixed spice (page 144)
- ½ teaspoon (2.5 g) baking soda
- Pinch (0.25 g) of salt
- ½ cup (90 g) coconut oil, melted
- ⅓ cup (100 g) maple syrup
- Pecan halves, for topping

1. Preheat the oven to 400°F. Line a baking sheet with parchment paper.
2. Combine all the dry ingredients in a bowl and mix well. Add the melted oil and maple syrup and stir them in.
3. Divide and shape the mixture into tablespoon-size balls and place them on the baking sheet.
4. Flatten each ball with the damp palm of your hand to about ½ inch thick and top each one with half a pecan.
5. Bake for 12 to 13 minutes until the cookies turn golden around the edges.
6. Let the cookies cool and firm up on the baking sheet for 5 to 10 minutes, then transfer them to a wire rack. Don't try to pick them up straightaway as cookies made with almond meal are more crumbly.

NUTRITION NOTE

Botanically pecans are fruits and although they're high in calories, they're also nutritionally great across the spectrum. Find any excuse you can to use pecans!

THE ULTIMATE CHOCOLATE COOKIES

MAKES 30 small cookies

EQUIPMENT cookie cutters, baking sheet

These small, crunchy cookies are perfect for when you're looking for a quick but intense chocolate hit. They were an immediate hit with our customers, too.

The cacao nibs add an extra, crunchy dimension to the already delicious chocolaty taste.

- ¾ cup (1½ sticks/170 g) unsalted butter, at room temperature
- 1 cup (packed) (200 g) coconut sugar
- Pinch (0.25 g) of salt
- 2 egg yolks
- 3 tablespoons (45 g) coconut oil, melted
- 1½ cups (200 g) spelt flour
- Scant 1¼ cups (120 g) raw cacao powder
- Cacao nibs, for topping

1. Beat together the butter, sugar, and salt by hand or using electric beaters until light and fluffy. Add the egg yolks and oil and beat them in. Finally, add the flour and cacao powder and beat until it all combines into a dough.

2. Flatten the dough into a disk, wrap it in plastic wrap, and chill in the refrigerator for at least an hour. This dough will also keep for up to 5 days in the refrigerator.

3. Preheat the oven to 400°F. Line a baking sheet with parchment paper.

4. Remove the dough from the refrigerator and roll it out to about 1/8 inch. Cut out the cookie shapes, sprinkle them with cacao nibs, and place them on the baking sheet.

5. Bake for 12 to 14 minutes. Let the cookies cool and firm up on the sheet for 5 to 10 minutes, then transfer them to a wire rack.

NUTRITION NOTE

Cacao is high in iron, which helps our brain and immune system to function. It also helps to reduce tiredness and fatigue.

GINGER AND TURMERIC SOURDOUGH COOKIES

MAKES 8 cookies
EQUIPMENT baking sheet

These sourdough cookies may have similar spices to our other ginger cookies, but that's where the similarity ends. They're soft and indulgent with a nice chewy outer crust and the gorgeous ocher glow that only turmeric delivers.

DAY 1

- Scant 1/4 cup (30 g) (packed) coconut sugar
- 1/4 cup (30 g) spelt flour
- 2 tablespoons whole milk
- Active Sweet Starter (page 184)

Add the sugar, flour, and milk to the whole quantity of Active Sweet Starter and leave loosely covered overnight at room temperature.

DAY 2

- 3 1/4 ounces (90 g) recipe starter from Day 1
- 1/4 cup (50 g) coconut oil, melted and cooled
- Generous 1/3 cups (75 g) (packed) coconut sugar
- 1 teaspoon vanilla extract
- 2/3 cup (60 g) almond meal
- 1/3 cup (60 g) spelt flour
- 1/2 teaspoon (2.5 g) ground cinnamon
- 1/4 teaspoon (1 g) ground turmeric
- 1/4 teaspoon (1 g) ground black pepper
- 1 teaspoon (5 g) ground ginger
- 1/2 teaspoon (2.5 g) baking soda
- Pinch (0.25 g) of salt

1. Preheat the oven to 400°F and line a baking sheet with parchment paper.
2. In a bowl, mix together the recipe starter, oil, sugar, and vanilla.
3. In another bowl, combine the almond meal and flour with the spices, baking soda, and salt.
4. Add the flour mix to the starter mix and stir well. The mixture will have the consistency of a loose dough.
5. Place eight tablespoon-size balls of the dough onto the baking sheet. Leave plenty of room between them as they will spread during baking.
6. Bake for 12 to 15 minutes. The cookies should be crispy around the edges but still soft in the middle. Let them cool on the baking sheet. Store in an airtight container for up to 5 days.

CHOCOLATE CHIP SOURDOUGH COOKIES

MAKES 8 cookies **EQUIPMENT** baking sheet

☰

These cookies are our version of an American chocolate chip cookie. They are delicious and gooey and will satisfy any urges you may have in the cookie aisle in the grocery store.

DAY 1

- Scant ¼ cup (30 g) (packed) coconut sugar
- ¼ cup (30 g) spelt flour
- 2 tablespoons (25 g) whole milk
- Active Sweet Starter (page 184)

Add the sugar, flour, and milk to the whole quantity of Active Sweet Starter and leave loosely covered overnight at room temperature.

DAY 2

- 3¼ ounces (90 g) recipe starter from Day 1
- ¼ cup (50 g) coconut oil, melted and cooled
- Generous ⅓ cup (75 g) (packed) coconut sugar
- 1 teaspoon (5 g) vanilla extract
- ⅔ cup (65 g) almond meal
- Generous ⅓ cup (50 g) spelt flour
- 1¾ ounces (50 g) coconut sugar–sweetened chocolate or your favorite healthy chocolate, chopped into chunks
- ½ teaspoon (2.5 g) baking soda

1. Preheat the oven to 400°F and line a baking sheet with parchment paper.
2. In a large bowl, mix the recipe starter with the oil, sugar, and vanilla.
3. In another bowl, combine the almond meal, flour, chocolate chips, and baking soda.
4. Add the flour mix to the starter mix and stir well. The mixture should have the consistency of a loose dough.
5. Place eight tablespoon-size balls of the dough onto the baking sheet. Leave plenty of room between them as they will spread during baking.
6. Bake for 12 to 15 minutes. The cookies should be crisp around the edges but still soft in the middle. Let cool on the baking sheet, then store in an airtight container for up to 5 days.

NUTRITION NOTE

These cookies may look like and taste like a typical chewy cookie, but because the core ingredients have been fermented and they have no refined sugar, their GI levels are much lower than that of a store-bought version, which can contain additives and preservatives.

CHEESY STICK SOURDOUGH COOKIES

≡

These gorgeous savory cookies take no time at all to make. They are a great example of how home-baked gluten-free products do not have to compromise on taste! We use our brown rice gluten-free starter in these and find that it complements the flavor of the cheese incredibly well.

DAY 1

- Scant ¼ cup (25 g) brown rice flour
- 2 tablespoons (25 g) water
- Active Gluten-Free Brown Rice Starter (page 42)

Add the flour and water to the whole quantity of active starter, mix, and leave loosely covered overnight at room temperature.

DAY 2

- 1¾ ounces (50 g) recipe starter from Day 1
- 6 tablespoons (85 g) unsalted butter, softened
- ½ cup (50 g) grated strong cheese (we recommend cheddar or Gruyère), and a little extra for topping
- ½ cup (55 g) buckwheat flour
- ½ cup (50 g) tapioca flour
- ¼ cup (25 g) almond meal
- 2 teaspoons (10 g) chopped fresh chives
- Pinch (0.25 g) of salt and a generous pinch (0.25 g) of ground black pepper

1. Preheat the oven to 400°F and line a baking sheet with parchment paper.
2. In a large bowl, combine all the ingredients and bring them together with your hands until they form a dough.
3. Let chill in the refrigerator for 20 minutes as this will make the dough easier to handle.
4. Roll out the dough on a floured counter and cut into sticks, approximately ½ inch wide.
5. Place the cookies on the baking sheet and sprinkle with the extra grated cheese. Bake for 15 minutes until a light golden brown. Let cool on the sheet.
6. Store in an airtight container for up to 5 days.

MAKES 15 cookies **EQUIPMENT** baking sheet **GF**

SOURDOUGH RYE CRACKERS

MAKES about 10 crackers

EQUIPMENT baking sheet

DF V+

≡

It's worth making a sourdough starter for these fabulous crackers alone. They're so easy to make, and incredibly versatile. We like to cut them into long rectangles for dipping in hummus, small triangles for cheese, and broken up for croutons in soups or salads.

We often top them with a sprinkling of seaweed flakes for more umami kick, but they're equally delicious sprinkled with sesame seeds or mixed dried herbs. You can play around with any different combinations you like.

DAY 1

- Scant ¼ cup (50 g) warm water (90 to 99°F)
- ½ cup (50 g) light rye flour
- Active Rye Starter (page 42)

Add the water and the rye flour to the whole quantity of the active starter, mix well, and leave loosely covered overnight at room temperature.

DAY 2

- 3½ ounces (100 g) recipe starter from Day 1
- 1 cup (125 g) white bread flour
- Scant ¾ cup (75 g) light rye flour
- Scant ¼ cup (50 g) olive oil
- Scant ¼ cup (50 g) warm water (90 to 99°F)
- Pinch (0.25 g) of salt
- Sesame seeds, dried herbs, or seaweed flakes, for sprinkling

1. Preheat the oven to 425°F and line a baking sheet with parchment paper.
2. In a bowl, mix all the ingredients together until they form a dough.
3. Roll the dough out very thin (about 1/16 inch) and cut into long rectangular strips.
4. Prick the strips with a fork, transfer them to the sheet, and sprinkle with seaweed, sesame seeds, or dried herbs.
5. Bake for about 15 minutes, turning occasionally, until they are crisp and golden.
6. Transfer the crackers to a wire rack until completely cool. Store in an airtight container for up to 2 weeks.

LIFE-CHANGING CRACKERS

MAKES 30 crackers **EQUIPMENT** 2 baking sheets, food processor, 2-inch round cutter **GF** **DF**

≡

These crackers are based on one of our gluten-free loaves inspired by Sarah Britton of *My New Roots*, one of our food heroes.

Psyllium husks are an astonishingly good source of dietary fiber and are available in most health food stores. And with so many nuts and seeds you can imagine how much "crunch" these little crackers have. We like to spread them with smoked hummus, avocado, or simply butter.

NUTRITION NOTE

Seaweed has become increasingly popular lately. Its natural sodium content can be used as an alternative to salt in recipes and it brings other nutritional benefits. We like to use a Shony seaweed flake as it has quite a light flavor, but you can play around with whichever type of flake you like best.

- ½ cup (70 g) sunflower seeds
- ⅓ cup (40 g) flaxseeds
- ¼ cup (35 g) hazelnuts
- ¾ cup (70 g) oats
- 2 teaspoons (10 g) chia seeds
- 1 ounce (25 g) psyllium husk
- ½ teaspoon (2.5 g) salt
- 1 teaspoon (5 g) seaweed flakes
- 2 tablespoons (25 g) coconut oil, melted
- 1 tablespoon (15 g) runny honey

1 Preheat the oven to 325°F. Line two baking sheets with parchment paper.

2 In a food processor, blitz all the dry ingredients until the sunflower seeds, oats, and hazelnuts are the texture of sand. Don't worry if the flaxseeds and hazelnuts don't grind down; they provide a nice texture to the crackers.

3 Add 2/3 cup (150 ml) water, oil, and honey to the food processor and blitz again until the mixture comes together and there are no dry patches.

4 Turn out onto a work counter and rest for 5 minutes. The dough will be easier to work with.

5 Roll the dough out to approximately 1/16 inch thick. Cut out the crackers with a 2-inch round dough cutter. Continue rolling and cutting until all the dough has been used up.

6 Place the crackers on the baking sheets—they can be close together but shouldn't be touching.

7 Bake for 30 minutes, then turn them over. Bake for another 15 minutes, or until an even golden brown.

8 Let cool on the sheet, then store them in an airtight container for up to 2 weeks.

PEANUT BUTTER OAT BARS

MAKES 8 bars
EQUIPMENT 10½ × 8-inch brownie tray
GF DF

This is one of our most popular oat bars—there's even a following for the broken bits!

The peanut butter and quinoa not only complement the sweetness of the honey, they also add extra protein, which is important because that's what keeps you feeling fuller for longer. No empty carbs in these bars.

We use smooth peanut butter, but you can use crunchy if you prefer it. Both are easy to make in a high-speed blender like a Vitamix. You can also play around with your choice of nuts; we often change these bars by using chopped cashews and almonds instead of peanuts, or a mixture.

- Generous 1 cup (250 g) smooth peanut butter
- ½ cup (150 g) runny honey
- 2 tablespoons (25 g) coconut oil
- Scant 1 cup (175 g) cooked quinoa
- 1 cup (100 g) oats
- ⅔ cup (50 g) dry unsweetened coconut
- ¾ cup (100 g) peanuts, roasted but not salted, chopped
- 3 tablespoons (25 g) sesame seeds

1. Preheat the oven to 400°F and line a 10½ × 8-inch brownie tray with parchment paper.

2. In a small pan, gently heat the peanut butter, honey, and oil until the oil has melted and they are easy to mix together. Let cool slightly.

3. In a bowl, mix together the cooked quinoa, oats, dry unsweetened coconut, and chopped nuts. Pour the peanut butter mixture over the top and combine well.

4. Pour the mixture into the tray, press down well, smooth the surface, and top with the sesame seeds.

5. Bake for 20 minutes until golden brown. Let cool in the tray, then turn out onto a cutting board and cut into eight pieces.

NUTRITION NOTE

As peanuts are high in fat, they are often viewed as unhealthy, but they contain the healthy fats that help to reduce the risk of cardiovascular disease.

SOURDOUGH OAT BARS

MAKES 8 bars

EQUIPMENT 10½ × 8-inch brownie tray

GF DF V+

≡

As soon as we'd made our first batch of sourdough granola, we immediately thought how amazing a sourdough oat bar would be, and so this recipe was born. We make these bars with golden raisins and hazelnuts because they create such a classic taste with the vanilla, but you can adapt the added ingredients to your taste. Try different nuts, seeds, and fruit, or some coconut sugar-sweetened chocolate chips for a real treat.

DAY 1

- Generous 1 cup (240 g) warm almond milk
- 2 cups (200 g) oats
- 1 tablespoon coconut sugar
- Active Oat Starter (page 266)

Add the milk, oats, and sugar to the whole quantity of the Active Oat Starter and leave loosely covered overnight at room temperature.

DAY 2

- 16 ounces (460 g) recipe starter from Day 1
- ½ cup (100 g) coconut oil, melted
- ⅓ cup (100 g) maple syrup
- 2 teaspoons (10 g) vanilla extract
- 2 cups (200 g) oats
- ¾ cup (100 g) golden raisins
- ¾ cup (100 g) hazelnuts
- 1 teaspoon (5 g) ground cinnamon
- Pinch (0.25 g) of salt
- Pumpkin seeds, for decoration

1. Preheat the oven to 400°F and line a 10½ × 8-inch brownie tray with parchment paper.
2. In a large bowl, mix together the recipe starter, melted oil, maple syrup, and vanilla.
3. In another bowl, mix together the oats, golden raisins, hazelnuts, cinnamon, and salt.
4. Gradually add the dry mix to the wet mix and combine thoroughly. Doing this gradually makes it much easier to combine, as the oat starter can make it quite stiff.
5. Empty the mixture into the brownie tray. Pack it down well and top with the pumpkin seeds.
6. Bake for 30 minutes until golden brown. Let cool completely in the tray, then turn out onto a cutting board and cut into eight bars.

TAHINI AND OLIVE OIL OAT BARS

☰

We return here to one of our favorite baking combinations, tahini (sesame seed paste) and olive oil. We sometimes throw in a small handful of goji berries or anything else we want to try out. If you're anything like us, you won't be able to resist buying new ingredients you come across.

The sweetness comes from the deep, rich flavor of maple syrup. And the quinoa, almond meal, and sesame seeds enhance the nuttiness.

- ⅔ cup (150 g) light tahini (sesame seed paste)
- ⅔ cup (150 g) olive oil
- ⅓ cup (100 g) maple syrup
- 1 teaspoon (5 g) vanilla extract
- ½ cup (100 g) cooked quinoa
- 1¾ cups (165 g) oats
- ½ cup (50 g) almond meal
- 5 heaping tablespoons (50 g) sesame seeds, plus more for topping
- Pinch (0.25 g) of salt

1. Preheat the oven to 400°F and line a 10½ × 8-inch brownie tray with parchment paper.
2. In a bowl, mix together the tahini, olive oil, maple syrup, and vanilla.
3. In another bowl, combine the cooked quinoa, oats, almond meal, sesame seeds, and salt.
4. Add the tahini mix to the oat mix and thoroughly combine.
5. Pour the mixture into the pan, pack it down really well, and sprinkle with sesame seeds.
6. Bake for 30 minutes until an even golden brown all over. Let cool in the tray and once completely cool, turn out onto a cutting board and cut into eight bars.

NUTRITION NOTE

Tahini is a great nutrient powerhouse for vegans as it contains calcium, zinc, and iron, which are all nutrients that can be hard to get hold of in a vegan diet.

MAKES 8 bars **EQUIPMENT** 10½ × 8-inch brownie tray **GF** **DF** **V+**

APPLE AND POPPY SEED OAT BARS

MAKES 8 bars **EQUIPMENT** 10½ × 8-inch brownie tray **GF** **DF**

≡

We often use banana to bind our oat bars, but as our job is to innovate, we created this rather different bar, using apple instead. The apple gives a lighter, less dense feel, but just as delicious. The cardamom, ginger, and vanilla work really well with the apple, which by the time it's grated and cooked isn't a dominant flavor.

Even a tiny quantity of poppy seeds always adds great visual impact. The little black dots always make their presence known, both visually and in the little crunch they bring. When I eat these I'm forever checking to see if the poppy seeds are stuck in my teeth!

- ⅓ cup (100 g) honey
- Scant ⅓ cup (60 g) coconut oil
- Generous 3 cups (300 g) oats
- Scant ⅔ cup (75 g) black poppy seeds
- Pinch (0.25 g) of salt
- ½ teaspoon (2.5 g) ground cardamom
- 1 teaspoon (5 g) ground ginger
- 2 apples, unpeeled, cored, and grated
- 1 teaspoon (5 g) vanilla extract

1. Preheat the oven to 400°F. Line a 10½ × 8-inch brownie tray with parchment paper.

2. In a small pan, melt the honey and oil together.

3. In a large bowl, combine the oats with the seeds, salt, and ground spices. Add the melted oil and honey mix, apples, and vanilla to the oats and spices. Mix well until there are no dry patches.

4. Pour into the prepared pan and press down well.

5. Bake for 30 minutes until the top is golden and the edges are turning slightly brown. Let cool in the pan, then turn out and cut into eight bars.

NUTRITION NOTE

Poppy seeds are nearly 50 percent omega-6, a valuable unsaturated fatty acid, and although there's not a huge quantity per portion in this recipe, there are nonetheless measurable amounts of fiber.

ALMOND BUTTER PROTEIN OAT BARS

☰

We sell a lot of oat bars to people who enjoy their exercise and they particularly like them when we've added some extra protein. There are many varieties and brands of protein powder—in this recipe we've used a pumpkin and chia one—but feel free to use whatever you like, but keep an eye on quality.

- ½ cup (125 g) almond butter
- ¼ cup (50 g) coconut oil
- ½ cup (150 g) date syrup
- ½ cup (100 g) cooked quinoa
- Scant 1⅔ cups (155 g) oats
- 2 tablespoons (25 g) pumpkin and chia protein powder
- 1 teaspoon (5 g) vanilla extract
- Scant ⅔ cup (50 g) slivered almonds
- 3½ tablespoons (25 g) sunflower seeds
- 3½ tablespoons (25 g) pumpkin seeds

1. Preheat the oven to 400°F and line a 10½ × 8-inch brownie tray with parchment paper.
2. In a pan, gently heat the butter, oil, and date syrup until the oil is completely melted and it all mixes together easily.
3. In a bowl, combine the cooked quinoa, oats, protein powder, vanilla, almonds, and seeds. Add the almond butter mixture and mix well.
4. Pour the mixture into the pan and pack down well. Bake for 25 minutes until it is a reddish golden brown all over. Let cool in the tray, then turn out and cut into eight bars.

NUTRITION NOTE

The quinoa, nuts, and seeds add an extra protein punch on top of the protein powder, and the oats and date syrup replenish your energy supplies.

MAKES 8 bars **EQUIPMENT** 10½ × 8-inch brownie tray **GF DF V+**

RAW BITES

MAKES 18 bites   EQUIPMENT 10½ × 8-inch brownie tray and a food processor   GF DF V+

≡

These could not be simpler to make, and they are beyond delicious. Once you have the basic recipe you can create infinite varieties. We make four standard flavors of raw bite in the bakery, and each month we have a special as well, such as a raw bite with wheatgrass, lemon, and honey, or a very popular chocolate, orange, and spirulina bite.

I took ten bites on a long-haul vacation recently, and could write a whole blog post about how they saved the day on many an occasion. These are the ultimate in healthy baking.

CHOCOLATE RAW BITES

- Scant 2 cups (140 g) dry unsweetened coconut
- 2½ cups (250 g) almond meal
- 2¼ ounces (60 g) chia protein powder
- ½ cup (150 g) maple syrup
- 2 tablespoons (25 g) coconut oil
- ¾ cup (75 g) raw cacao powder

RASPBERRY RAW BITES

- Scant 2 cups (140 g) dry unsweetened coconut
- 3 cups (300 g) almond meal
- 2¼ ounces (60 g) chia protein powder
- ½ cup (150 g) maple syrup
- 2 tablespoons (25 g) coconut oil
- 2 tablespoons (25 g) freeze-dried raspberry powder

Chocolate, raspberry, and matcha green tea are pictured on the left.

PEANUT BUTTER RAW BITES

- Scant 2 cups (140 g) dry unsweetened coconut
- 2½ cups (250 g) almond meal
- 2¼ ounces (60 g) chia protein powder
- ½ cup (150 g) maple syrup
- 2 tablespoons (25 g) coconut oil
- ⅔ cup (150 g) peanut butter

MATCHA GREEN TEA RAW BITES

- Scant 2 cups (140 g) dry unsweetened coconut
- 3 cups (300 g) almond meal
- 2¼ ounces (60 g) chia protein powder
- ½ cup (150 g) maple syrup
- 2 tablespoons (25 g) coconut oil
- 2 tablespoons (25 g) matcha green tea powder

1. Line a 10½ × 8-inch brownie tray with parchment paper.
2. Put all the ingredients for whichever bites you are making in a food processor and blitz until the mixture comes together. Empty into the prepared tray and smooth down well.
3. Place in the refrigerator for at least 4 hours, then turn out onto a cutting board and cut into 18 pieces.
4. These keep well in an airtight container in the refrigerator for up to 2 weeks or in the freezer for up to a month. Defrost for 1 to 2 hours in the refrigerator before eating.

RAW OAT BITES

MAKES 8 large or 16 small bites

EQUIPMENT 10½ × 8-inch brownie tray and a food processor

GF DF V+

≡

These oat bites are not baked. They are bound by dates rather than honey or maple syrup. This is another easy recipe to tweak. For example, you could make them with dried apricots instead of dates, almonds instead of walnuts, and mixed spice or even fresh ginger.

- 3¼ cups (440 g) pitted dates
- ½ cup (100 g) coconut oil, melted
- 1 tablespoon (15 g) maca powder
- Scant 2 cups (180 g) oats
- 2 teaspoons (10 g) vanilla extract
- 1 teaspoon (5 g) ground ginger
- 1 teaspoon (5 g) ground cinnamon
- ½ cup (50 g) coarsely chopped walnuts

1. Line a 10½ × 8-inch brownie tray with parchment paper.
2. In a food processor, blend together the dates, ½ cup (120 g) water, and oil until they form a relatively smooth paste, with no big pieces of date remaining.
3. In a large bowl, mix together the rest of the ingredients. Add the date mixture and use your hands to combine into an even dough with no dry patches.
4. Empty the dough into the tray and spread out evenly. Chill in the refrigerator for at least 4 hours, then turn out and cut into 8 or 16 pieces. These keep well in the refrigerator for up to 2 weeks or in the freezer for up to 1 month. Defrost for 1 to 2 hours in the refrigerator before eating.

NUTRITION NOTE

As well as the slow carb release that oats bring, these bars are packed with goodness: maca has been shown to help with energy and endurance, and cinnamon to help the oats do an even better job.

SOURDOUGH GRANOLA

≡

The idea for sourdough granola came from a conversation about the benefits of soaking grains before eating them because it enhances the grain's nutritional profile. Lindsay was then asked, "If you soak oats overnight, could you go farther and make sourdough oatmeal?" That idea is still in development, but it sparked the thought that an oat-based sourdough granola could be delicious. It turns out it definitely is!

We make the starter with almond milk, but you can use any nut or dairy milk.

⇢ Pictured overleaf

OAT STARTER

DAY 1

- Scant ¼ cup (20 g) oats
- 2 tablespoons (25 g) almond milk, at body temperature
- 1 teaspoon (5 g) coconut sugar

Mix all the ingredients together in a container with a lid. We recommend mixing with your hands rather than a spoon. We all have naturally occurring yeasts on our hands, so this can give your starter a real boost.

Leave the mixture overnight at room temperature. Cover it with the lid but do not make it airtight. A screw-top jar with the lid partly done up is perfect. You want the yeasts in the air to get in, but you also want to stop the mixture from drying out.

DAY 2

- Oat Starter made on Day 1
- Scant ¼ cup (20 g) oats
- 2 tablespoons (25 g) warm almond milk
- 1 teaspoon (5 g) coconut sugar

Throw away half the mix from Day 1 and add the oats, milk, and coconut sugar to the remaining mix. Stir well and leave loosely covered at room temperature overnight.

NUTRITION NOTE

The sourdough element will provide the digestive tract with good bacteria, which is especially beneficial at breakfast, and all the nuts and seeds will help to keep you off the snacks until lunchtime.

MAKES about 4½ pounds granola

EQUIPMENT container with a lid and a rimmed baking sheet or roasting pan **GF DF V+**

DAYS 3 AND 4

Repeat Day 2.

DAY 5

- Oat starter made on Day 4
- Generous 2 cups (200 g) oats
- Generous 1 cup (260 g) warm almond milk
- Scant ¼ cup (40 g) (packed) coconut sugar

1. By now your starter should feel like it has some activity in it; it should have air bubbles and we find that it smells slightly gluelike. This is completely normal and in no way indicates what the final granola tastes like, so don't panic. If your starter still seems sluggish, repeat Day 2 until it activates.

2. Add the oats, milk, and sugar, mix well, and leave loosely covered overnight at room temperature.

DAY 6

- 1 pound (500 g) oat starter from Day 5
- ⅓ cup (100 g) maple syrup
- ¾ cup (150 g) coconut oil, melted
- Generous ¾ cup (100 g) unsalted cashews
- 1¼ cups (100 g) slivered almonds
- 1 cup (150 g) mixed seeds of your choice
- Scant 7 cups (650 g) oats
- 1½ tablespoons (22.5 g) ground cinnamon
- Scant 1 cup (100 g) dried goji berries

1. Preheat the oven to 400°F and line a deep-sided cookie sheet or roasting pan with parchment paper.

2. In a bowl, combine the recipe starter, maple syrup, and oil.

3. In another bowl, mix together the dry ingredients, except for the goji berries.

4. Add the dry mix to the wet mix and stir really well; you might want to get into the mix with your hands as it can be quite stiff. Make sure there aren't too many big lumps.

5. Spread the mix evenly on the cookie sheet. Bake for 30 minutes, then stir to break up any big pieces. Bake for another 15 minutes, then stir again. Bake for another 15 minutes.

6. At this point the granola should be baked through and starting to become golden. If you like your granola dark, then return it to the oven for another 5 minutes, otherwise remove it from the oven and let cool completely on the cookie sheet.

7. Stir through the goji berries (never bake these, as they will burn) and store in an airtight container for up to a month.

COCONUT, NUT, AND SEED GRANOLA

MAKES 3¼ pounds granola
EQUIPMENT rimmed baking sheet or roasting pan
GF DF V+

≡

Over Modern Baker's lifetime we have tried out a few different granolas but this one, the very first we made, has proved by far the most popular. We have customers who take it with them all over the world, from Switzerland to the summit of Kilimanjaro. It is delicious on its own as a snack, with yogurt at breakfast, or with a banana, almond milk, and spinach as a smoothie.

Pictured on previous spread

- 6 cups (300 g) coconut flakes
- Scant 1¼ cups (150 g) Brazil nuts
- 1⅓ cups (170 g) almonds
- 1⅓ cups (150 g) unsalted cashews
- Generous 1 cup (150 g) pecans
- 1 cup (150 g) sunflower seeds
- 1 cup (150 g) pumpkin seeds
- ¼ cup (30 g) ground flaxseeds
- ½ cup (110 g) coconut oil
- ½ cup (160 g) maple syrup

1. Preheat the oven to 400°F and line a deep-sided cookie sheet or roasting pan with parchment paper.
2. In a large bowl, mix together the coconut, nuts, and seeds.
3. In a small pan, melt the oil with the maple syrup over medium heat.
4. Add the oil and maple syrup to the nut mix and combine thoroughly.
5. Turn the mixture out on the baking sheet and spread out evenly.
6. Bake for 15 minutes, then stir to break up any big pieces. Return to the oven for 7 minutes, then stir again. Return to the oven for a final 7 minutes. At the end the granola should be an even, golden brown.
7. Let the granola cool on the baking sheet, then store in an airtight container for up to 2 weeks.

CHRISTMAS GRANOLA

MAKES 4½ pounds granola
EQUIPMENT rimmed baking sheet or roasting pan

GF DF V+

≡

This tweak of our house granola (left) evokes all the seasonal flavors associated with Christmas. It makes a great gift, and a lovely way to introduce friends and family to healthier eating.

- 6 cups (300 g) coconut flakes
- 1⅓ cups (170 g) almonds
- 1¼ cups (150 g) hazelnuts
- 1¼ cups (150 g) unsalted cashews
- 1 cup (150 g) sunflower seeds
- ¼ cup (60 g) ground flaxseed
- 1 tablespoon (15 g) ground cinnamon
- 1 teaspoon (5 g) mixed spice (page 144)
- 1 teaspoon (5 g) ground nutmeg
- ½ cup (110 g) coconut oil
- Scant 1 cup (180 g) maple syrup
- 1 teaspoon (5 g) vanilla extract
- Zest of 1 orange, grated
- ⅔ cup (100 g) chopped dried figs
- Scant 1 cup (100 g) dried goji berries
- Scant 1 cup (100 g) dried cranberries

1. Preheat the oven to 400°F and line a deep-sided cookie sheet or roasting pan with parchment paper.
2. In a large bowl, mix together the coconut, nuts, seeds, and spices.
3. In a small pan, melt the oil with the maple syrup, vanilla, and orange zest.
4. Add the wet mixture to the dry mixture and combine thoroughly.
5. Pour the mixture into the prepared baking sheet and bake for 15 minutes. Stir to break up any large pieces and return to the oven for another 7 minutes. Stir again, then return to the oven for a final 7 minutes. The final granola should be an even golden brown all over.
6. Let the granola cool on the baking sheet, then stir through the dried fruit and store in an airtight container for up to 2 weeks.

NUTRITION NOTE

The greater the variety of ingredients in your diet the better, and with sixteen in this you'd be hard pressed to beat this recipe on that score.

GLOSSARY

BANANA FLOUR
Made from green bananas, this contains lots of fiber. It doesn't taste of bananas when cooked. It has a low glycemic index and is gluten-free.

BARBERRIES
A small, sweet, and slightly sour dried berry, popular in Iranian cooking. More tart than a cranberry. Goji berries or raisins can be used as an alternative.

CACAO NIBS
Cacao is the purest form of chocolate that's edible. Completely unprocessed, it contains everything that's good about chocolate. The nibs are the crushed and roasted pieces of the whole bean, and offer a wonderful crunch in baking.

CHESTNUT FLOUR
Made by finely milling chestnuts, this works particularly well when combined with other gluten-free flours. It gives a delicious nutty flavor as well as providing a good source of fiber.

CHIA SEEDS
Tiny poppylike seeds, come black or white, a staple of healthy cooking for high nutrition. Used for their crunch and appearance in food or their useful gelatinous quality when soaked.

COCONUT SUGAR
From the sap of the coconut palm, it has a much lower glycemic index than refined white and brings lovely flavors to baking.

FLAXSEED
These small brown seeds are uber healthy and appear frequently in our recipes, both ground and whole.

GOJI BERRIES
A healthy food scene star for a long time now, these small orange-red berries, high in antioxidants and texture, are really versatile in modern-day cooking.

LUCUMA
The powdered yellow flesh of a South American sweet fruit, it's a great for sweetening cakes and smoothies with a high fiber content. This tastes a bit like maple syrup.

MACA
A caramel-tasting powder derived from the root of the maca plant from the high Andes, used for its nutrition benefits as well as flavor.

MAPLE SYRUP
The sap of the maple tree is one of the most popular natural sweeteners available, and easy to use in baking. It adds color and a rich flavor.

MATCHA POWDER
A finely milled vibrant green powder made from high-quality Japanese green tea leaves. It is highly nutritious and brilliant for coloring cakes, cookies, and hot drinks.

MILLET
Millet is a high-fiber and gluten-free tiny seed grown all over the world and used in just about every type of cooking. It comes as a hulled seed or as flour, both of which are used in baking.

MORINGA
Used in Ayurvedic medicine for thousands of years, it's a high-protein, high-fiber green leaf powder from South Asia that works well in baking.

NUT AND SEED MILKS
Sometimes referred to as mylks to differentiate them from dairy milk. A vast range is now available in most grocery stores and most are interchangeable in recipes. We use almond, brown rice, coconut, and cashew nut.

PROTEIN POWDERS
Derived from various plant ingredients such as pea, brown rice, hemp, chia, and more. Quality varies widely so always do your homework. These are very easy to include in baking.

PSYLLIUM HUSKS
This is made from the husk of a plantago seed milled into a grainy powder. Great for gluten-free baking as it helps bind the other ingredients because it acts as a gel when wet.

RASPBERRY POWDER
Made from freeze-dried, powdered raspberries, it's a really useful pantry ingredient for both flavor and color—and is a winner for healthy frostings.

SAUERKRAUT
Shredded cabbage and salt, left to ferment in a deoxygenated environment for a few weeks. Extraordinarily rich in gut-friendly bacteria, we increasingly use it in savory baking.

SEAWEED
An increasingly popular ingredient due to its nutrition levels, and used as an alternative to salt in some cooking. It comes in many forms but it's mainly the dried flakes that are used in baking.

SPIRULINA
A naturally occurring alga, dried and ground into a fine, dark green powder and packed with nutrients. Needs to be used with care because of its strong flavor but a very useful ingredient in healthy baking.

TURMERIC
Arguably one of the most significant spices for better health, the fine, golden powder brings an earthy taste to baking but also pairs well with sweet flavors. There are few better natural food colorings available.

INDEX

A

almond butter
· almond butter protein oat bars 260
· apple and almond butter cake 161
apples:
· apple and almond butter cake 161
· apple and cider sourdough 68–70
· apple and poppy seed oat bars 258–9
· apple and sourdough bread pudding cake 170
· apple, rose, and walnut big cake 126
· apple sourdough cake 192–3
· carrot, apple, and walnut cake 147
· orchard cake 144
arugula:
· roast butternut squash, goat cheese, walnuts, arugula, and pomegranate pizza 116
avocados:
· avocado, feta, black olive, red onion, and oregano tartine 87
· chocolate and avocado ganache 215
· chocolate, avocado, and millet cake 168–9

B

bacon:
· Brussels sprouts, coconut bacon, feta, and hazelnuts tartine 87
banana flour:
· sweet potato and banana flour cake 140
bananas:
· banana, cinnamon, and lucuma cake 164
· raw banoffee pie 211
barberry cake, tangy 138–9
beer:
· whole grain rye and beer sourdough 84
beet:
· beet and sauerkraut sourdough 58–9
· raw beet, strawberry, and coconut cake 208–10
the big cake 124–31
blackberries, rye sourdough with raspberries and 86–7
blondies, sourdough peanut butter 196
blueberries:
· maple sugar and blueberry scones 178–9
bread 26–116
· basic techniques 30–5
bread pudding cake, apple and sourdough 170
breakfast friands 172
broccoli and Stichelton sourdough 56–7
brownies, quinoa 182
Brussels sprouts, coconut bacon, feta, and hazelnuts tartine 87
buns 102–9
butternut squash, goat cheese, walnuts, arugula, and pomegranate pizza 116

C

cakes 118–227
carrots:
· carrot and walnut sourdough cake 194–5
· carrot, apple, and walnut cake 147
· carrot, cumin, and Gouda loaf cake 226–7
· Melissa's life-changing carrot and olive oil cake 122–3
· raw carrot cake 206–7
cashews:
· vanilla cashew nut frosting 214
chai tea, orange, and cranberry sourdough 64
cheese:
· avocado, feta, black olive, red onion, and oregano tartine 87
· broccoli and Stichelton sourdough 56–7
· carrot, cumin, and Gouda loaf cake 226–7
· cheesy stick sourdough cookies 248
· olive and feta sourdough 52
· roast butternut squash, goat cheese, walnuts, arugula, and pomegranate pizza 116
· rosemary, parsnip, and Parmesan loaf cake 224
· spinach, yogurt, and goat cheese loaf cake 223
cheesecakes 198–200
chestnut flour:
· coffee, chocolate, and chestnut cake 146
· plum, chestnut, and black pepper cake 165

chia seeds:
· golden lucuma and chia cookies 239
· raspberry chia jam 219
· superloaf with chia and quinoa 71–2
chickpea flour 25
· gluten-free chickpea sourdough 94
chiles:
· lime, chile, and cinnamon big cake 130
chocolate:
· chocolate and avocado ganache 215
· chocolate and ginger tart 204
· chocolate and pear slice 175
· chocolate, avocado, and millet cake 168–9
· chocolate chip sourdough cookies 246–7
· chocolate cream cheese frosting 218
· chocolate, hazelnut, and raisin spelt sourdough 78–9
· chocolate moringa cake 134–5
· chocolate raw bites 263
· chocolate sourdough cake 186–7
· coffee, chocolate, and chestnut cake 146
· gluten-free chocolate, raisin, and hazelnut sourdough 99
· quinoa brownies 182
· raw millionaire's shortbread 202–3
· raw peanut butter and chocolate cups 212–13
· the ultimate chocolate cookie 244
Christmas granola 271
cider:
· apple and cider sourdough 68–70
cinnamon:
· banana, cinnamon, and lucuma cake 164
· cinnamon cookies with pecan halves 243
· lime, chile, and cinnamon big cake 130
· sourdough cinnamon and pecan buns 102–4
coconut:
· Brussels sprouts, coconut bacon, feta, and hazelnuts tartine 87
· coconut and lime cake 156
· coconut, nut, and seed granola 270
· completely coconut loaf cake 150–1
· parsnip and coconut cake 171
· raw beet, strawberry, and coconut cake 208–10
coconut milk:
· coconut and lemon curd sourdough buns 108–9
coffee:
· coffee and pecan nut cake 142–3
· coffee, chocolate, and chestnut cake 146
coffee cream cheese frosting 216
cookies 228–48
crackers 250–3
cranberries:
· chai tea, orange, and cranberry sourdough 64
cream cheese:
· chocolate cream cheese frosting 218
· coffee cream cheese frosting 216
· lemon cream cheese frosting 219
· maple cream cheese frosting 216

D

dried fruit:
· breakfast friands 172
· Christmas granola 271
· Simnel cake 158–60
· sourdough granola 266–7

E

Earl Grey tea and peach sourdough 64
eggplant:
· roasted eggplant, pesto, and tomato pizza 116
equipment 36–7

F

fig upside-down cake with lucuma 154–5
flatbreads, gluten-free sourdough 96
flours 22, 25
focaccia 75
· sourdough focaccia 74–5
folding 32–3
friands 172–4
frostings 208, 214–19
fruit cakes: fruity friands 174
· Simnel cake 158–60

G

ganache, chocolate and avocado 215
ginger:
· chocolate and ginger tart 204
· ginger and pepper spicy cookies 238
· ginger and turmeric sourdough cookies 245
· ginger sourdough cake 190
· rhubarb and ginger cheesecake 200
gluten-free bread 35
· gluten-free sourdough 90–5, 98–100
· gluten-free sourdough flatbreads 96
· gluten-free sourdough pizza base 112
gluten-free flours 25
gluten-free starters 42
golden raisins:
· green tea, lemon, and golden raisin sourdough 63–4
granola:
· Christmas granola 271
· coconut, nut, and seed granola 270
· sourdough granola 266–7
green tea *see* matcha green tea

H

hazelnuts:
· Brussels sprouts, coconut bacon, feta, and hazelnuts tartine 87
· chocolate, hazelnut, and raisin spelt sourdough 78–9
· gluten-free chocolate, raisin, and hazelnut sourdough 99
honey:
· golden turmeric and honey cookies 236

I/J

ingredients, measuring 30
jam, raspberry chia 219

K

kale and feta scones 222

L

lemon curd:
· coconut and lemon curd sourdough buns 108–9
lemons:
· black olive and lemon sourdough focaccia 75
· green tea, lemon, and golden raisin sourdough 63–4
· lemon cream cheese frosting 219
· lemon sourdough cake 188
· matcha and lemon big cake 125
· matcha green tea and lemon cheesecake 200
· matcha green tea and lemon scones 181
life-changing crackers 252–3
lime:
· coconut and lime cake 156
· lime, chile, and cinnamon big cake 130
loaf cakes 150–2, 222, 225–7
lucuma:
· banana, cinnamon, and lucuma cake 164
· fig upside-down cake with lucuma 154–5
· golden lucuma and chia cookies 239

M

maca and vanilla cake 136
maple sugar and blueberry scones 178–9
maple syrup:
· maple cream cheese frosting 216
marzipan 158–9
matcha green tea:
· bright green matcha cookies 242
· green tea, lemon, and golden raisin sourdough 63–4
· matcha and lemon big cake 125
· matcha green tea and lemon cheesecake 200
· matcha green tea and lemon scones 181
· matcha green tea raw bites 263
Melissa's life-changing carrot and olive oil cake 122–3
millet:
· chocolate, avocado, and millet cake 168–9
millionaire's shortbread, raw 202–3
Modern Baker basic sourdough 44–7
Modern Baker Victoria sponge 132–3
moringa powder:
· chocolate moringa cake 134–5
multiseed sourdough 48–50

N

nuts:
· coconut, nut, and seed granola 270
· gluten-free nutty sourdough 95

O

oats:
· almond butter protein oat bars 260
· apple and poppy seed oat bars 258–9
· oat starter 244
· peanut butter oat bars 254
· raw oat bites 264
· sourdough oat bars 255
· tahini and olive oil oat bars 256
olive oil:
· Melissa's life-changing carrot and olive oil cake 122–3
· tahini and olive oil cookies 235
· tahini and olive oil oat bars 256
olives:
· avocado, feta, black olive, red onion, and oregano tartine 87
· black olive and lemon sourdough focaccia 75
· olive and feta sourdough 52
oranges:
· chai tea, orange, and cranberry sourdough 64
· turmeric and orange big cake 125
orchard cake 144

P

parsnips:
· parsnip and coconut cake 171
· rosemary, parsnip, and Parmesan loaf cake 224
peaches:
· Earl Grey tea and peach sourdough 64
peanut butter:
· peanut butter cheesecake 200
· peanut butter oat bars 254
· peanut butter raw bites 263
· raw peanut butter and chocolate cups 212–13
· sourdough peanut butter blondies 196
pears:
· chocolate and pear slice 175
· orchard cake 144
pecans:
· cinnamon cookies with pecan halves 243
· coffee and pecan nut cake 142–3
· sourdough cinnamon and pecan buns 102–4
· zucchini and pecan loaf cake 152
pesto:
· roasted eggplant, pesto, and tomato pizza 116
· savory pesto and walnut sourdough buns 105–6
· seaweed pesto tear and share sourdough 60–2
pita bread, sourdough 110–11
pizza, sourdough 112–16
· gluten-free 112
plum, chestnut, and black pepper cake 165
pomegranates:
· roast butternut squash, goat cheese, walnuts, arugula, and pomegranate pizza 116
poppy seeds:
· apple and poppy seed oat bars 258–9
proofing 32–3, 34

Q

quinoa flour 25
· quinoa brownies 182
· superloaf with chia and quinoa 71–2

R

raisins:
· chocolate, hazelnut, and raisin spelt sourdough 78–9
· gluten-free chocolate, raisin, and hazelnut sourdough 99
· rye, caraway, and raisin sourdough 85
raspberries:
· raspberry chia jam 219

· raspberry raw bites 263
· rye sourdough with raspberries and blackberries 86–7
· vanilla and raspberry cheesecake 198–9
rhubarb and ginger cheesecake 200
rice flour 25
· gluten-free brown rice starter 42
rosemary:
· rosemary, parsnip, and Parmesan loaf cake 224
· sweet potato and rosemary sourdough 54–5
rose water:
· apple, rose, and walnut big cake 126
rye flour 22, 35
· rye, caraway, and raisin sourdough 85
· rye seeded sourdough 81–2
· rye sourdough 80–1
· rye sourdough with raspberries and blackberries 86–7
· rye starters 42
· sourdough rye crackers 250
· wholegrain rye and beer sourdough 84

S

sauerkraut:
· beet and sauerkraut sourdough 58–9
scones 179–81, 224
scoring 34
seaweed:
· salty sweet seaweed cookies 232–3
· seaweed pesto tear and share sourdough 60–2
seeds:
· coconut, nut, and seed granola 270
· gluten-free seeded sourdough 92–3
· multiseed sourdough 48–50
· rye seeded sourdough 81–2
shaping bread 33
shortbread, raw millionaire's 202–3
Simnel cake 158–60
sourdough 18, 44–70, 78–86
· apple and sourdough bread pudding cake 170
· gluten-free sourdoughs 90–100
· sourdough buns 102–9
· sourdough cakes 184–96
· sourdough cookies 244–8
· sourdough focaccia 74–5
· sourdough granola 266–7
· sourdough oat bars 255
· sourdough pita bread 110–11
· sourdough pizza 112–16
· sourdough rye crackers 250
· sourdough starters 40
spelt flour 22
· chocolate, hazelnut, and raisin spelt sourdough 78–9
spinach:
· spinach and spirulina sourdough 88
· spinach, yogurt, and goat cheese loaf cake 223
sprouted grains 22, 66
· sprouted whole wheat sourdough 66–7
starters 40–2
strawberries:
· raw beet, strawberry, and coconut cake 208–10
· strawberry and pink peppercorn big cake 129
sugar, natural 21
superloaf with chia and quinoa 71–2
sweet potatoes:
· sweet potato and banana flour cake 140
· sweet potato and rosemary sourdough 54–5

T

tahini:
· tahini and olive oil cookies 235
· tahini and olive oil oat bars 256
tartines 89
tart, chocolate and ginger 204
temperature 35
tigernut cookies 234
tomatoes:
· cherry tomato, basil, and avocado oil focaccia 75
· gluten-free sundried tomato and basil sourdough 100
· roasted eggplant, pesto, and tomato pizza 116
· tomato sauce 113
turmeric:
· ginger and turmeric sourdough cookies 245
· golden turmeric and honey cookies 236
· turmeric and orange big cake 125

U

the ultimate chocolate cookie 244
upside-down cake, fig 154–5

V

vanilla:
· maca and vanilla cake 136
· vanilla and raspberry cheesecake 198–9
· vanilla cashew nut frosting 214
Victoria sponge, Modern Baker 132–3

W

walnuts:
· apple, rose, and walnut big cake 126
· carrot and walnut sourdough cake 194–5
· carrot, apple, and walnut cake 147
· roast butternut squash, goat cheese, walnuts, arugula, and pomegranate pizza 116
· savory pesto and walnut sourdough buns 105–6
· walnut sourdough 51
wheat 22, 41
· sprouted whole wheat sourdough 66–7
whole grain rye and beer sourdough 84

Y

yogurt:
· spinach, yogurt, and goat cheese loaf cake 223
· yogurt frosting 218

Z

zucchini:
· zucchini and pecan loaf cake 152

SUPPLIERS & STOCKISTS

BAKING EQUIPMENT
www.williams-sonoma.com
www.nycake.com

GROCERIES
www.wholefoodsmarket.com
www.seaveg.com
www.amazon.com

FLOURS
www.arrowheadmills.com
www.amazon.com
www.bluebirdgrainfarms.com
www.tigernutsusa.com

BOOKS

- *At Home in the Whole Food Kitchen* by Amy Chaplin
- *Gut* by Giulia Enders
- *How to Make Bread* by Emmanuel Hadjiandreou
- *Nourishing Traditions* by Sally Fallon
- *Stirring Slowly* by Georgina Hayden
- *The Art of Fermentation* by Sandor Ellix Katz
- *The Diet Myth* by Professor Tim Spector
- *Under the Walnut Tree* by Anna Bergenstrom

ABOUT US

MODERN BAKER is a successful organic, sourdough bakery and café in Oxford. But that's just one part of our ambitious business. We set up the café as a "proof of concept," to test out our ideas about fermentation and health, to establish our brand, and to help us understand the healthy food business. Through the store, every day we meet and serve hundreds of customers, many of them fanatical about what we stand for, but we have also attracted attention from the most unexpected quarters: schools who want to go "sugar-free"; a university with a vision to put a sustainable heart into a huge building project; private equity firms who find that specialty baking has found its way into the Top 10 of businesses to invest in; a major grocery store that would like to have a slice of healthy baking; and restaurants who want us to pop-up with a fermented menu.

Modern Baker is growing. As I write we are setting up The Kitchen, an off-site bakery capable of producing up to one thousand loaves a day. This will allow us to wholesale Modern Baker branded products through other retailers and online. The Kitchen site also includes an R&D and consultancy division.

We're always being asked whether we're opening up further retail outlets, and plans are afoot to do so.

Most exciting for us, though, is the substantial funding award we've received from the UK's innovation agency, Innovate UK. This will cofund a two-year project supporting our vision to further improve the nutritional qualities of our sourdough breads and other baked goods, while making them available to a much wider public. We will be collaborating with academic researchers, food scientists, Public Health, and all sides of the agricultural community to examine, amend, and quantify our natural baking processes in line with government targets on lowering salt, sugar, and fat in the major food groups, while increasing fiber levels.

It seems very fitting somehow that we're applying modern science to a technology that's been around for tens of thousands of years—fermentation. Indeed, it was the technological platform that in many ways created modern man. This is why we call ourselves Modern Baker.

WWW.MODERNBAKER.COM

THANK YOU

A few years ago if anyone had said I'd be writing a book, I'd have responded with equal parts laughter and panic. But one thing I've learned is that life has no recipe. You just have to keep trying things out.

One thing's for sure: if not for my cancer there would be no book, as there'd be no Modern Baker. But while I'm genuinely grateful for the gift of adversity, most of my thanks are reserved for the people who've been by my side throughout the voyage.
First, without both Lindsay and Leo there would be neither Baker nor book. Lindsay brought talent and tenacity while Leo added love, support, and business vision. Both have been more central than anyone can imagine.

Every single member of our team has contributed to this book, whether recipe testing or just taking the strain. I also want to thank Ashley for her help with some of the recipes and for her solid support; Mary for keeping us on the ball with all the rules and regulations about nutrition; Annie, Laura, and Polly for their creativity; Bo Bo and Silla dog walks for lightening heavy burdens; Modern Baker's longest front of house, Katharine, for her friendship and reliability; Lizzy and Iris for being among our favorite customers; my lovely friend Anne Marie for her constant moral support and encouragement; Charlotte for her quirky illustration and Tim for getting the brand across with fewer words than I could ever seem to manage; Robyn for helping coordinate the content; Caroline and everyone at Felicity Bryan Associates for inspiring us to do this; Sandra and the team at Ebury for pulling this together; my dad for teaching me a good value system and my mom for letting me "flour" the kitchen after school! And finally my lifelong friends Jo, Craig, and Vanessa for their constant belief and encouragement.